Scottish Embroidery
MEDIEVAL TO MODERN

Scottish Embroidery

MEDIEVAL TO MODERN

MARGARET SWAIN

B.T. BATSFORD Ltd   London

For Kathleen Whyte DA, MBE

© Margaret Swain 1986
First published 1986

All rights reserved. No part of this publication
may be reproduced, in any form or by any means,
without permission from the Publisher

ISBN 0 7134 4638 2

Typeset by Servis Filmsetting Ltd, Manchester
and printed in Great Britain by
Butler & Tanner Ltd
Frome Somerset
for the publishers
B.T. Batsford Ltd
4 Fitzhardinge Street
London W1H 0AH

The publisher and the author gratefully acknowledge
subsidy from the Scottish Arts Council towards the
publication of this volume.

Contents

List of Illustrations   6

Acknowledgements   9

Introduction   10

1. Before the Reformation   12
2. The Queen's Embroiderers   19
3. Mary, Queen of Scots   32
4. The Professional Embroiderer in the Seventeenth Century   41
5. The Domestic Needlewoman in the Seventeenth Century   53
6. Domestic Embroidery in the Eighteenth Century   68
7. Tambouring and Ayrshire Embroidery   93
8. Scottish Samplers   107
9. Victorian Embroidery   123
10. The Glasgow School of Art   138
11. Talented Amateurs   153
12. The New Professionals   171

Appendix I: Embroideries for the Church of Scotland designed and worked by staff and students of the Glasgow School of Art   183

Appendix II: Places to see Scottish embroidery mentioned in this book   186

Index   187

Illustrations

Black and white

1. Chalice veil.
2. Detail of the Fetternear Banner.
3. The White Banner of Mackay.
4. Linlithgow Hanging.
5. Lochleven Hanging.
6. Campbell of Glenorchy valance.
7. Detail: *The Temptation.*
8. Detail: *The Expulsion from Paradise.*
9. Woodcut published in Venice 1486.
10. Sketch of stitch.
11. Arniston panel, detail.
12. Campbell of Glenorchy valance.
13. Valance: *Daniel Rescued from the Lions' Den.*
14. Engraving: *Daniel Rescued from the Lions' Den.*
15. Engraving, Antwerp 1565.
16. Engraving: *Mary, Queen of Scots.*
16a. Signature of Mary, Queen of Scots.
17. Octagon panel: MARIE STVART.
18. Central panel, the Marian Hanging.
19. Cruciform panel: DELPHIN.
20. Woodcut: *The Dolphin,* 1555.
21. Cruciform panel: A PHESANT.
22. Woodcut: *A Pheasant,* 1560.
23. Panel: Royal Arms of James I.
24. Detail of panel.
25. Portrait: *John Drummond, Earl of Melfort,* Kneller.
26. Mantle of the Order of the Thistle, 1687.
27. Lord Chancellor of Scotland's Purse.
28. Lord Rollo's Standard, 1689.
29. The Spalding Banner.
30. Portrait: The Earl of Wemyss in Archer's uniform, 1736.
31. Bonnet, worn by the Earl of Wemyss.
32. Engraving, detail. *The Riding to Parliament, Edinburgh.*
33. Herald's tabard, with the Arms of Scotland, 1707–1714.
34. Detail, crewel work bed hanging, 1640.
35. Bed cover from Cullen House.
36. Detail of Cullen House bed cover.
37. Painted and dyed hanging, India 1675–1725.
38. Detail of a crewel work bed hanging.
39. Crewel work bed valance.
40. Panel from velvet bed hangings, decorated with 'slips'.
41. Detail from the same bed hangings.
42. Pelmet of wall hangings at Glamis.
43. Detail of Glamis hangings.
44. Unfinished panel of 'slips' at Traquair.
45. Canvas work cockerel, applied to velvet curtain.
46. Large panel: *The Finding of Moses.*
47. Close-up of pot of flowers on a bed curtain at Wemyss Castle.
47a. Key to fig. 47.
48. Chair with fish-scale carving, 1756.
49. Chair with cover in rice stitch, at Drum.
50. Settee with needlework cover.
51. Portrait: *Henrietta, Duchess of Gordon,* attributed to P. Mercier, c.1750.
52. Firescreen, initialled *H G,* 1754.
53. Wall hanging, signed 'Anne Grant 1750'.
54. Sketch: elevation of a room by Robert Adam.
55. Wall panel from Newliston.
56. Drawing Room, Newliston.
57. Portrait: *Lady Mary Hog,* attributed to David Allan.
58. Part of a pelmet, wool appliqué.
59. Two panels of a screen.
60. Double-faced embroidery on paper – *colifichet.*
61. Portrait: *Matilda, wife of General James Lockhart* attributed to G. Knapton, 1788.
62. Portrait: *Jane, Countess of Hopetoun,* Gainsborough.
63. Portrait: *Elizabeth, Countess of Hopetoun,* Gainsborough.

64. Design for a lappet, Henrietta Cumming.
65. Corner design for embroidery, c.1761.
66. Corner of a fichu in drawn muslin.
67. Sketch of a commercial tambouring frame.
68. Detail of a tambour work sampler.
69. Portrait: *Mrs Jamieson*, of Ayr.
70. Worker's sampler of lace stitch fillings.
70a. Detail of sampler in fig. 70.
71. Baby robe of Ayrshire embroidery.
72. Detail of the hem of a baby robe.
73. Baby's cap of Ayrshire embroidery.
74. Crown of the cap in fig. 73.
75. Multiplication table sampler.
76. The Mellerstain Panel, 1706.
77. Engraving: 'Smelling', from the '*Five Senses*'.
78. Page from *A Booke of Beast*, 1630.
79. Sampler, Elizabeth Gardner, 1818.
80. Sampler, Elizabeth Gardner, 1820.
81. Sampler, Elizabeth Gardner, 1821.
82. Sampler, Elizabeth Gardner, 1822.
83. Sampler, Catherine McDonal, 1822.
84. Engraving: *Inverary Castle*, 1759.
85. Sampler, Mary Butler Stark, 1803
86. Sampler, Janet Learmonth, 1765.
87. Memorial sampler, Agnes Currie, 1833.
88. Panel for a carpet, Berlin wool work.
89. Screen panel: *The Scottish Gamekeeper*.
90. Trade sampler, Mrs & Miss Bowie, Edinburgh, c.1860
91. Embroidered blanket initialled *IC*, 1705.
92. *The Royal Clothograph Work of Art*.
93. Theatrical print: T.P. Cooke in *Black Ey'd Susan*.
94. White embroidered monogram, 'Angela'.
95. Lap quilt of cream satin.
96. Panel: *The Entrance*, Phoebe Traquair, 1895.
97. Photograph of Mrs Newbery (Jessie Rowat).
98. Unfinished tea-cosy by Jessie Newbery.
99. Cushion cover by Jessie Newbery.
100. Illustration: children's clothes by Jessie Newbery.
101. Photograph of Ann Macbeth.
102. Panel: *The Nativity*, Ann Macbeth.
103. Panel: *The Little Visitor*, Kathleen Mann, 1937.
104. Hanging: *Icarus*, Kathleen Whyte.
105. Pulpit fall, Marilyn McGregor.
106. Panel, Ian Black, 1980.
107. Lenten pulpit fall, Chrissie White, 1980

108. Bed embroidered by the Countess of Strathmore, Glamis Castle.
109. Cushion from furnishings worked by the Countess of Strathmore.
110. Bed cover worked by Constance, Countess of Crawford.
111. Carpet (detail) by Mary, Countess of Dalhousie.
112. White panel: *The British Royal Arms*, by Lady Evelyn Stuart Murray, c.1912.
113. Sketch: design for a bed cover, Sir Robert Lorimer.
114. Detail of bed cover for Kellie Castle.
115. Photograph of Maggie Hamilton (Mrs A.N. Paterson).
116. Panel: *Doves and Clematis*, Maggie Hamilton, c.1900.
117. Three kneelers for the chapel at Falkland Palace.
118. Stall cushion for the Abbey Church of Iona.
119. Square of *lacis* (darned net, or *filet brodé*), 1930.
120. Tea cosy in ribbon work, 1933
121. Part of a hanging, *The Jedforest Hunt*, 1960.
122. Detail, showing the embroideress and her sister.
123. Blackwork panel: *Chimneys*, Margery Hyde, 1970.
124. Embroidered box: *Pandora's Box*, Anna Younger.
125. Photograph of Louisa M. Chart in her studio, 1938.
126. Canvas work panel: *The Royal Burgh of Edinburgh*, 1938.
127. The Cardross Panels, Hannah Frew Paterson.
128. Detail of the right-hand panel in fig. 127.
129. Canvas work panel: *Field II*, Veronica Togneri, 1978.
130. Panel: *Night Sky*, Jennifer Hex, 1983.
131. *Highland Triptych (Torridon)*, Alison King, 1984.
132. Collage: *The World of Poultry*, Inga Blair, 1981.
133. Panel: *King Tod*, Mary Johnstone.

Colour

I. The Fetternear Banner.
II. Silk embroidered panels, Campbell of Glenorchy.
III. Badge of the Thistle Robe.
IV. Detail of panel at Traquair.
V. Detail of an embroidered curtain, 1729.
VI. Firescreen: *The Sacrifice of Isaac*.

VIa. Engraving: 'The Sacrifice of Isaac', *c*.1660.
VII. The Newliston Bed, on loan to the Georgian House, Edinburgh.

VIII. Sampler, Margret Boog, 1761.
IX. Two panels, Margaret Macdonald, 1902.
X. The Mayfield Frontal, Kathleen Whyte, 1972.

Acknowledgements

Over the years, many people have helped me trace the history of Scottish embroidery. Since 1947, when I first had the good fortune to come to live in Scotland, owners, museum curators and librarians, too many to be named, but most gratefully remembered, have been generous in sharing their knowledge, and this book reflects something of what I have learned from them.

The idea of a book devoted to Scottish embroidery originated with Kathleen Whyte. To her I owe a deep debt of gratitude for encouragement and advice, especially in regard to the development of modern embroidery, a development in which she herself has played a distinguished part. Her successor at the Glasgow School of Art, Crissie White, has been equally generous in supplying me with details of the history of the School.

I am deeply grateful to HM the Queen for gracious permission to reproduce the needlework settee and the firescreen at the palace of Holyroodhouse, and to all the other owners who have allowed objects, many still in the houses for which they were made, to be photographed. Naomi Tarrant, of the Royal Museum of Scotland,

has supported and advised me during the writing of this book, and Hugh Cheape, at the same establishment has given generous assistance. Brian Blench and Elizabeth Arthur of the Kelvingrove Museum, Glasgow, as well as Christopher Hartley and John Batty of the National Trust for Scotland and Ian Gow, of the Royal Commission on the Ancient and Historical Monuments of Scotland, have each contributed expertise, and I offer them my warmest thanks. Dr Rosalind Marshall of the National Portrait Gallery of Scotland, and Dr Helen Bennett, have given me friendship as well as scholarly advice. I owe a great deal to the staff of the National Library of Scotland and the Scottish Record Office for their patient help in my search to find out who made these embroideries, and where the materials and designs were obtained in the past. Finally, my affectionate thanks are due to my sister, Isabel Miller, who helped me with the typescript.

No bibliography is included, but for students and others, full references are given at the end of each chapter.

Introduction

There remains in Scotland such a wealth of needlework from the past that it seems surprising that no book has so far been published dealing solely with Scottish embroidery and embroiderers.

Some of the most notable examples – the panels of Mary, Queen of Scots now at Oxburgh Hall, Norfolk, and the delicate whitework known as Ayrshire embroidery – usually figure in histories of English embroidery, though both are outside the mainstream of English traditional needlework. The first is entirely Franco-Scottish in its conception, the other a highly successful development of an exacting technique applied to a locally produced fabric: the fine cotton muslin spun and woven in the west of Scotland.

It is, however, unrealistic to search for a distinctive Scottish style, since Scotland, as well as England, was a part of Europe, and sensitive to the same fashions and tastes. But history, and their relative geographical positions, affected the balance of such influences. Until James VI of Scotland succeeded Elizabeth in 1603 to become James I of Great Britain, the kingdoms of England and Scotland were two separate and often warring nations. It was not until the union of the two parliaments of Scotland and England in 1707 that the two nations were politically united. Before that date Scotland looked to France for support against its more powerful neighbour, especially in the sixteenth century, cementing the alliance with royal marriages which culminated in the brief union of the two kingdoms when the young Mary, Queen of Scots was also the Queen Consort of France.

Scottish ties with the Netherlands went back long before the Dutch William III claimed the throne of Great Britain in 1688. Scottish ships exported coal and hides to the Netherlands where, in the port of Veere, preferential treatment was extended to Scottish ships and merchants. They brought back among their cargoes choice textiles, especially fine linen, often named after their country of origin: *holland*, *cambric* and *dornick*, a linen damask, after Tournai.

Scotland, like the Netherlands, adopted the reformed religion of Calvinism and resisted, often with violence, attempts to impose the Lutheran customs of bishop and prayer book adopted by the Church of England. Instead, the Scots clung to the Presbyterian order, sending their students to universities on the continent, especially in the Netherlands, to maintain their independence.

Until 1700, therefore, Scottish taste in embroidery was more likely to be influenced by France or the Netherlands, rather than England. Only after 1707, when the two parliaments were united in Westminster, were English fashions widely adopted. Travel between the two capitals, Edinburgh and London, became easier, though it must be remembered that until the laying of the railways in the 1840s, bulky goods such as furnishings, as well as many passengers, had to be transported by sea rather than by land. It was necessary therefore for native embroiderers, both professional and domestic, to rely upon their own resources for designs and materials, though letters show how eagerly they sought news of the latest fashion.

Even in so small a matter as making buttons for her husband's ruffles, the Scotswoman was sometimes driven to invention, as Lady Nairne, writing to the Countess of Panmure in 1705, explained:

Last time I writt to your Ladyship I forgot to tell you that I think I've found the true way of making the thread buttons. I send a couple enclos'd . . . The want of moulds at Dunkeld and the reading in the votes of the English Parliament about the bean and berry button makers put me upon my invention to find out what was meant by it. I now make the moulds of the half of a pea, which I either make myself or gets some of the idle men to do it for me and so saves the trouble of having moulds from wrights. One of those inclosed has a pea mould and I send to your Ladyship two without covers that if you like the contrivance you may see how 'tis done. The pea this button was made of is too little, but that Your Ladyship knows I think no fault for my Lord's hand wrists [ruffles].[1]

This book is not merely an account of the domestic needlewoman in Scotland, however delightful her work and comments. I have tried to show the part played by the professional embroiderer. This is not because the professional was more dominant in Scotland than in England. On the contrary, there was no Broderers' Company as in the City of London, nor, after 1600, any court or church to commission work. But with few exceptions, most accounts of British embroidery have so far ignored the part played by the professional, so that it is often assumed that any piece that has survived must be the work, and even the design, of a talented amateur. I hope what I have written may suggest a more balanced view.

References
1. SRO Dalhousie Muniments GD 45/14/245(a). I am indebted to Dr Rosalind Marshall for this reference.

CHAPTER ONE

Before the Reformation

In August 1560, the Scottish parliament, sitting in Edinburgh, established the Protestant reformed religion throughout Scotland. Their Queen, Mary, a Catholic, was still Queen of France, the wife of Francis II (who was to die four months later). Mary's mother, the Regent, had died in June. Unlike other European states, whose religion was imposed by the ruler, the Scots people at one stroke cut themselves off from their medieval past and took a decision which profoundly affected their thinking, their industry and their fiercely independent way of life.

Regrettably, this step also resulted in the total destruction of the needlework that had undoubtedly graced the churches and abbeys of Scotland in the previous centuries. The few fragments that remain owe their survival to accident. Outside the Chapel Royal of Holyrood (for the Scottish parliament respected the Catholic religion of their Queen), statues and vestments associated with the old religion were destroyed with a zeal and thoroughness unequalled in any other European country. The destruction of church needlework and silver was not always due to Calvinist iconoclasm, but partly the result of a shortage of cash and native thrift. Vestments and plate from the Kirk of St Giles, Edinburgh, had been distributed to members of the Burgh council for safe-keeping. In 1561, they had to be sold, probably for the gold and jewels on them, in order to pay the stipend of John Knox, the Calvinist reformer, now minister of the Kirk:

May 27 [the council ordained] The Kaipis [copes] Vestmentis and alter grayth [furnishings] quilk pertaineth to Sanct Gelys presentlie in handis or so far as may be gotten in, to be deliverit to David Somer, baillie, and to James Barroun, and they to dispone to the maist advantage. . . . The Baillies and haill counsall ordainis James Watsoun, dene of gyld, incontinent to deliver to Johne Knox, minister, the sowme of fyftie pundis for his quarter payment.[1]

Even Edinburgh's flag was not immune from reforming zeal. On 24 June 1562, the provost, baillies and council 'ordainis the idole Sanct Geyell [Giles] be cuttit forth of the townys standart and the thrissill [thistle] put in place thairof, and that the thesaurer furnis taffete to the samyn'.

It was not only the Reformers who destroyed church needlework. Even the Queen contributed to its destruction. On the death of her French husband, Mary, Queen of Scots returned to her own country, her personal Catholic faith respected by parliament. In 1562, the year that the offending image of St Giles had been excised from Edinburgh's standard, the rebel Earl of Huntly died in the battle of Corrichie, Aberdeenshire. The Queen presided over a grisly trial in Edinburgh, where his roughly embalmed body was tried for treason. His belongings were seized and sent from Aberdeen to Edinburgh, where they were carefully listed by the Queen's valet de chambre, Servais de Condé. They included copes, chasubles and other vestments, some thought to have been entrusted to the care of the Catholic earl by the provost and clergy of Aberdeen Cathedral for safe-keeping at the time of the Reformation two years previously.

There is no record of their being taken into use in the Chapel Royal. On the contrary, notes appended to the inventory show that they were cut up and used for furnishings. In the spring of 1565, there is noted: 'Three copes, two tunicles and a chasuble, all of green velvet, whose ornatments were broken up to decorate a bed with embroidery and flowers', with sufficient left over to cover a high chair, two seats and a *chaise percée* (commode). A cope, chasuble and four tunicles were all cut up in the Queen's presence, to make a bed for Darnley, her second husband, while in March 1567: 'I deliverit thre of the fairest quilk the Quene gaif to the Lord Bothwell' – her third husband, and a Protestant.

It becomes clear, therefore, how Scotland's store of medieval needlework perished. Instead, we have to rely on Court or Guild accounts for payment made to individual embroiderers, such as the wife of Gerard de Haustan, who embroidered the mortcloth of the Guild of Hammermen (metalworkers) in 1497, or a community of nuns, the Grey Sisters, who worked a corporal for them in 1512. There was also John Young, embroiderer to James V, who made a hanging for the Chapel Royal in 1540: 'Item, for the browdray and warkmanschip of thre Jesus wroucht with crown of thorn, three name of Jacobus quintus, with the kinge's armes and crown abone, the heid and twa unicorns berand the samin vii li. [£7].'[2]

Unlike England, its larger, wealthier neighbour, Scotland had no professional workshops of the quality of those in the city of London[3] that produced Opus Anglicanum, the superb needlework of silk and silver, which quite rightly commanded respect and high prices throughout the continent of Europe. The Netherlands, rather than England, provided the inspiration, if not the actual materials, for the decoration of Scottish church textiles before the Reformation.

Thus, in the lodging of Adam Colquhoun, Canon of Glasgow Cathedral, there was in 1542 an oratory, his private chapel, with two altar coverings of 'holland clayth', damask curtains, a frontal and chasuble of black velvet with gold orphreys, and a small velvet cushion on which lay the Canon's 'orasone buke coverit with green velvet', valued at twenty pounds.

The furnishings of his Hall showed that he lived in pleasing comfort. He had a case of knives, twelve small, three with broader blades, and even a fork, the ultimate refinement, all of them 'ourgilt with gold'. There was a (side) board cloth 'of dornick work, double' (double linen damask from Tournai), two dozen serviettes of dornick work, in addition to other napery, kept in an 'ark' or cupboard. Eleven coverings 'for ye counter' were listed, and a dozen 'fyne great cushinges of flanderis werk', probably woven tapestry. There was also a cope hood of silver, no doubt richly embroidered, and the glimpse of a secular pastime in the item: 'Ane schuting gluf sewit with silk, knoppit with gold . . . price XX marks' (a shooting glove for bow and arrow, embroidered with silk and embellished with gold buttons or tassels).[4]

The twelve fine great cushions remind us how necessary these decorative household furnishings must have been to soften the wooden seats of stools and settles before upholstered chairs came into general use. Sixty years later, in the well-furnished castle of Kenmure in Galloway, there were: 'Item, XI sewit kischings, with Flanderis worsett, and ten uther kischings, and XI that serves the hous dailie.'[5]

Even the royal palaces relied on cushions for comfort. In the inventory of 1578, there were ten chairs in Edinburgh Castle, nine velvet-covered and one covered with leather; also fourteen folding stools, two with seats of coloured embroidery, while no less than forty cushions were listed. These had covers of velvet, gilt, leather, sewed worsted, sewed silk and applied cloth of gold. Like the medieval church embroidery, all have perished.

The few pieces that may be said to be Scottish offer a tantalizing glimpse of the church embroidery of Scotland before the Reformation: fragments of altar frontals showing Flemish influence, and one or two chalice veils of fine linen. One (fig. 1), from the family of Drummond of Comrie, is bordered with a text embroidered in red silk, each

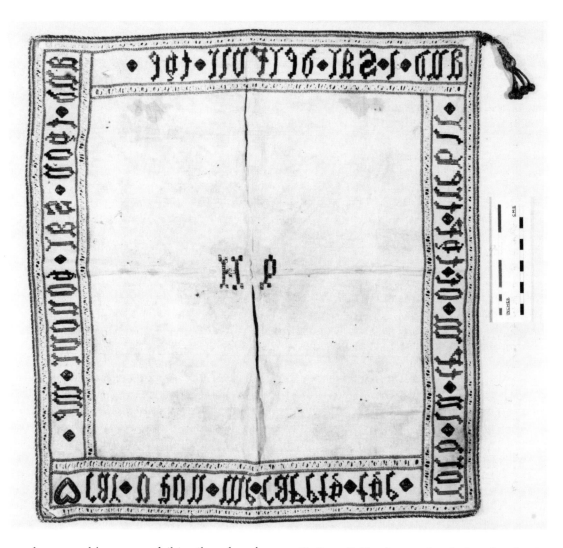

word separated by a quatrefoil in silver thread:

CAL . UPON . ME . CAYETH . THE . LORD . IN .
TYM . OF . THE . TREBIL .
AND . I . SALL . DELYVER . THE . AND . THOU .
SAL . HONOUR . ME .

(Psalm 50:15)

with the initials *H B* (or *P*) in the centre, perhaps the initials of the embroiderer.[6] Two others, now in the Scottish Record Office, are more modestly decorated. One shows a monstrance outlined in black, flanked by green candles. They owe their

1. Chalice veil. Fine linen with red silk embroidered lettering: 'CAL . UPON . ME . CAYETH . THE . LORD . IN . TYM . OF . THE . TREBIL . AND . I . SALL . DELYVER . THE . AND . THOU . SAL . HONOUR . ME,' with the letters H B *or* P *in the centre. 43.5 × 46 cm/17 × 18 in. (Trustees of the Royal Museum of Scotland)*

survival to the fact that they were made into covers for documents during the eighteenth century, and were preserved in drawers.[7]

The most outstanding example of pre-Reformation embroidery in Scotland is the Fetternear

Banner (colour plate 1), so called because it was given to the Roman Catholic church in Fetternear, Aberdeenshire, when it was built in 1859. (See also fig. 2.) It was presented by the laird, Colonel Charles Leslie, 26th Baron of Balquhain. Its previous history was unknown, but there was a legend that it had been carried by a Leslie in the battle of Pinkie in 1547. Instead, Monsignor David McRoberts[8] has demonstrated that the banner was laid away, unfinished and unused, some time between 1518 and 1522. It was made for the confraternity of the Holy Blood, who had an altar in the Kirk of St Giles, Edinburgh. It bears the arms of Gavin Douglas, the poet-bishop of Dunkeld, who translated Virgil into Scots. He was Provost of St Giles from 1503 to 1521. In that year he had been declared a rebel, and fled to England, where he died of the plague in 1522. His sudden death may have been the reason for the laying aside of the unfinished embroidery.

The panel is worked in brilliant silks on fine linen. It has no affinity with any English embroidery of the period; indeed, it has not been possible to find a comparable piece in Europe. The central design, the blood-flecked figure of the suffering Christ, surrounded by the Instruments of the Passion: the Cross, the scourge, the cock and dice, derives from German or Flemish art, particularly from the city of Bruges, devoted to the cult of the Sacred Blood. It was a city familiar to many Scottish merchants trading with the Low Countries, whence the linen must have come. The decorative borders have deep religious symbolism. The inner border shows the beads of the Rosary; the interlace of the middle border represents the *cordelière* or knotted cord worn by Franciscans and confraternities, while the unfinished outer border shows delicate flowers of columbine (symbolizing the Holy Ghost) and scallop shells, which figure in the embroidered arms of Alexander Graham, a furrier and burgess of Edinburgh. He was 'Kirkmaister' of the confraternity of the Holy Blood in Edinburgh in 1522, and may indeed have commissioned the banner.

It is not only the design of the banner that is outstanding, but its technique also. It is entirely double-faced, except for the letters *INRI* at the top of the T-shaped cross that cannot be reversed. Unlike the double-sided satin stitch found on Chinese embroideries, the Fetternear Banner is worked entirely in double running (Holbein) stitch, used as both outline and filling. No other instance of the stitch being used in this way as a filling is known in Britain, though it appears to be similar to a stitch used in Middle Eastern embroideries in the eighteenth century. This single Edinburgh piece, of such high quality, sharpens the sense of loss over the destruction of Scotland's store of ecclesiastical textiles.

The earliest Scottish embroidery so far discovered is neither ecclesiastical nor royal. It is a tattered banner of fine white silk, now darkened to fawn, and is embroidered with a lion rampant within a shield, worked in blue silk, and an open hand above, the fingers in yellow silk; it bears the Gaelic motto *Bi tren*: 'Be valiant' (in modern Gaelic *Bidh treun*). Around the hand runs the legend: 'Verk visly and tent to ye end'. (Fig. 3.)

The banner has a very respectable pedigree. First described by the Revd William McKenzie, of the parish of Tongue, in Sutherland, in the Old Statistical Account of 1793, it is believed to have descended from Ian Aberach, son of Angus Du Mackay by his second wife, daughter of Alexander Macdonald of Keppoch, and great-granddaughter of King Robert II. Ian Aberach is remembered for his leadership in the battle of Drum nan Coup in 1433. His eldest brother, by his father's first wife, was held a hostage of the king, his infirm father was carried on a litter, and Ian Aberach, still in his teens, led the Mackays in a decisive victory against the Sutherland men. In this period of clan warfare, the battle 'proved to be the Bannockburn of the Mackays . . . that saved their country from greedy and unnatural usurpers'.[9]

It is unlikely that this silken banner was ever carried in battle. It was probably made to hang in a hall, perhaps over a chair of estate. The leather casing at the top was made to receive a pole, by which it could be suspended. The heraldic details

do not accord with the Mackay arms as registered
with the Lyon King of Arms. But the Aberach
Mackays were a cadet branch, and apparently
never registered arms. In 1899 the Lyon King
observed guardedly: 'The whole flag is evidently
the work of someone unacquainted with the
principles of heraldic design.'

It has, however, been pointed out that the
'double tressure', or border, of the shield surrounding the lion rampant and decorated with
fleurs-de-lis, is a symbol of royal descent, to which
Ian Aberach was entitled through his mother. The
open hand appears on the arms of Mackay of
Strathnaven in 1503, but by the beginning of the
seventeenth century had become a closed hand
grasping a dagger.[10]

Certainly the heraldic details are crudely drawn.
The lion rampant with ferocious teeth and pro-
truding tongue, the silk of which has now perished,
accords with no known representation. The open
hand is primitive. This is not a design drawn out by
a court embroiderer. But the silk embroidery is
exceedingly assured, and worthy of better drawing. The banner is now framed and glazed,
preventing examination of the underside, but the

3. The White Banner of Mackay (Bratach Bhan
Chlann-Aoidh). Silk, originally white, embroidered in
blue and pale yellow silks in satin stitch. There is a
leather casing for a rod at the top. It shows a lion
rampant within a shield and an open hand with the
mottoes 'Verk visly and tent to ye end'; and Bi Tren
(Bidh treun: 'Be valiant'). Reputed to be the banner
of Ian Aberach Mackay, who fought in the battle of
Drum nan Coup in 1433. 74 × 44 cm/29 × 17½ in. (The
Clan Mackay)

design appears to be worked in satin stitch, perhaps double-sided, with great precision. This delicate piece gives a surprising glimpse of life in the remote and turbulent far north of Scotland in the fifteenth century.

References

1. Extracts from *Records of the Burgh of Edinburgh 1561*.
2. *The Accounts of the Lord High Treasurer of Scotland* vol. VII, p. 434.
3. Marc Fitch, 'London Makers of Opus Anglicanum', *Transactions of the London and Middlesex Archeological Society* vol. 27, 1976, pp. 288–92.
4. D. McRoberts, 'The Manse of Stobo. Inventory of effects of Master Adam Colquhoun, Canon of Glasgow and minister of Stobo, 1542,' *Innes Review*, Spring 1971, XXII (1).
5. 'Inventar of the Household Furniture of Kenmure after the death of Sir John Gordon of Lochinvar August 1604,' *Reliquae Antiquae Scoticae*, 1848.
6. Now in the Royal Museum of Scotland. *Proceedings of the Society of Antiquities of Scotland* LV.
7. Scottish Record Office Reg. Ho. Ch. 86c. Arbroath, Reg. Ho. Ch. 201b. Arbroath. They were found among papers brought back from the Scots College in Paris, dispersed at the time of the French Revolution.
8. D. McRoberts, 'The Fetternear Banner', *Innes Review*, Edinburgh, 1956, VII, p. 69. The fine linen and delicate silk embroidery appear rather fragile for use as a banner, even within the church, and it may have been intended as one of a pair of side curtains for the altar, though no tradition of decorated side curtains has been found.
9. Revd Angus Mackay, *The Book of Mackay*, Norman McLeod, Edinburgh, 1906.
10. Ibid. 'The Aberach-Mackay Banner', pp. 274–84. The banner is on loan to the Royal Museum of Scotland (L.1923.2a).

CHAPTER TWO

The Queen's Embroiderers

When the widowed Mary, Queen of Scots returned from France in 1561, she left behind one of the most brilliant courts of Europe. She found her own kingdom, over which she was to rule for seven brief years, impoverished by wars and dominated by a Puritan Kirk; the royal palaces shabby and uncomfortable after her mother's austere regency.

Mary brought with her a French *valet de chambre*, Servais de Condé, who made careful inventories of all the Queen's movables: the soft furnishings, sadly worn, left by her mother, and those that Mary had herself brought from France. He listed all materials issued to the three royal *tapissiers* (upholsterers rather than tapestry weavers) and the two professional embroiderers, Ninian Miller and Pierre Oudry. Miller was Scottish, but Oudry undoubtedly accompanied the Queen from France. He remained her devoted servant as long as she was in Scotland, and is believed to have followed her to England. The so-called Sheffield portrait of Mary, now at Hardwick Hall, is attributed to him.

The Queen brought in her luggage from France twenty beds (bedhangings and canopies, rather than the wooden bases, which were made of deal and hidden by the rich hangings). Twelve of these were embroidered, one in appliqué of satin in four colours, red, blue, yellow and white, bordered with 'false gold' and silver. Another, of crimson velvet, was embroidered with true lovers' knots and the cipher of her late husband, Francis II. Others, of velvet or satin, were sumptuously decorated with embroidery and appliqué. There were cushions and chair coverings as well as cloths of estate for the canopy under which the Queen sat to show her royal rank.

The lists show that throughout the Queen's stay in Scotland, new beds were continually being made, and old ones refurbished. Not all were embroidered, of course. Some were of woollen material, to keep out the cold, but others were richly decorated with appliqué of gold and silver, some of which came from cut-up vestments such as those seized from the Earl of Huntly. Gold, silver and silk threads were bought by the pound to embroider this handsome furnishing, as well as the Queen's clothes, made by her tailor. In October 1561 the Lord High Treasurer made payment for fourteen pounds eight ounces of black silk, a pound of 'sewing threid of gold', and 'ane pund wecht of sewing threid of silver', with three pounds by weight of 'violet armesie silk' (taffetas).[2]

In March 1565, ten double hanks of gold and silver were supplied at thirty-two shillings a hank, while in May the Treasurer paid for forty hanks of sewing gold weighing one pound eight ounces at sixteen shillings an ounce, six ounces of red silk at sixteen shillings an ounce, and six ounces of white silk at twelve shillings an ounce.[2]

That same year, a new bed was made from fifty-four yards of green and yellow damask, topped by 'ane knop ouregilt with gold to hang the pavilzeone' (a golden knob from which hung the canopy). For lining, twenty-two yards of 'grene armosene taffeteis' were needed, and one pound eight ounces of green and yellow silk for decoration, with three pounds of green worsted for fringes.[3] Clothing, heraldic work and repairs to existing embroidery all occupied the court embroiderers in activity that had been sadly neglected during the Queen's absence in France.

4. *The Linlithgow Hanging. Red woollen material, originally with a nap. Appliqué of black silk outlined and embellished with yellow silk embroidery.* 147.5 × 100 cm/57¾ × 39 in. (Trustees of the Royal Museum of Scotland)

The only pieces remaining from this rich flowering of court embroidery are hangings of black silk appliqué embroidered with yellow silk on a red woollen ground. There are two different designs, though both undoubtedly came from the same workroom. One, in the Royal Museum of Scotland, shows an heraldic lion at the base of a flowering tree, with a handsome border repeating the pineapple, pink and rose of the trees. This is believed to have come from the palace of Linlithgow. (Fig. 4.)

The other design, with similar ground and materials, came from the Bruce of Arnot family, who occupied Kinross House, overlooking the island castle of Lochleven where Mary was imprisoned for ten months before escaping to England. Inevitably a legend arose that this was the work of the Queen herself while on the island. One panel is in the Royal Scottish Museum of Scotland. Other surviving pieces of this so-called Lochleven Hanging (fig. 5) suggest that it was a set of wall hangings for a room. There are three pieces in a private collection, and two others at St Leonard's School, St Andrews.

All this court embroidery came to an end when Mary fled to England in 1568. Ninian Miller set up his own workshop in Edinburgh. Pierre Oudry left. The large frames were put away, to be stored with other gear, where they were listed in 1578 as 'Certane werklumes for ane brodinstare'.[4] Mary's son, James VI, still a child, was brought up in a Puritan atmosphere. William Beaton, Embroiderer to the King, did not work full time, but took on outside commissions. In 1582 he charged Jean Forbes, Lady Ogilivie, £40 Scots for 'ane hat string', an embroidered hat band, which she wore at her son's wedding.[5]

Private orders such as this and heraldic work for the Scots parliament must have provided work for those professional embroiderers with workshops in Edinburgh. Although embroidery was banished from the Kirk, and Presbyterian clothing was austere, needlework played an important part in bringing colour and warmth to the domestic interior. A bed continued to be the most important

5. The Lochleven Hanging, with valance and border. Red woollen material embellished and decorated as that in fig. 4. Other pieces of this design survive, suggesting that they were made as wall hangings. 180 × 112 cm/71 × 44 in. Valance: 25.6 × 142 cm/10 × 56 in. (Trustees of the Royal Museum of Scotland)

and expensive piece of furniture in the house. A number of valances, worked in silk and wool on canvas, have survived, many of them known to have come from Scottish castles, mostly around Perthshire, and all of them pieces of high quality. They are professionally drawn, and fall into three main types:

6. *Valance, from a set of three. Coloured wools and silks on canvas. The arms and initials are those of Sir Colin Campbell of Glenorchy and his wife, Katherine Ruthven, whom he married in 1550. 33 × 107 cm/13 × 43 in.* (The Burrell Collection, Glasgow)

7. BELOW *Detail of fig. 6: The Temptation. The serpent has a human face.*

8. OPPOSITE *Detail of fig. 6: The Expulsion.*

1. Biblical subject, professionally drawn, but probably home made.
2. Design showing a tree with an heraldic animal crouching at the base, as in the Linlithgow hanging.
3. Tent stitch valances showing figures wearing French costume, with Biblical or mythological scenes, some of them very obscure.

The first group is the best documented. Probably the earliest is the set of valances now in the Burrell collection, Glasgow, showing the arms of Sir Colin Campbell of Glenorchy, and of his second wife, Katherine Ruthven, whom he married in 1550. They had four sons and four daughters. He died in 1583 and since she was a second wife, it may be assumed that the valances were made soon after their marriage in 1550. (Figs. 6, 7, and 8.) All three valances show the Campbell arms; the shortest valance, for the foot of the bed, displays them impaling the Ruthven arms, with a true lovers' knot between the initials *C C* and *K R*, suspended from a ram's head, the Ruthven supporter. On either side are lively scenes of the temptation of Adam and Eve, and their expulsion from Paradise. These are probably taken from woodcuts in an early printed Bible. (Fig. 9.) Other motifs appear to derive from title pages or headings of books: mermaids, cupids astride a branch, the lion and unicorn. As bed valances, the three panels appear short, but they could, of course, have been mounted on a plain background for a large double bed. In 1640 no less than four beds at Balloch (now Taymouth Castle), were listed as bearing the arms and names of the Laird and Lady of Glenorchy on their valances.

These Campbell valances are noteworthy for the stitch employed. Although worked on canvas, it is not the usual tent stitch, but superficially appears to be chain stitch. Examination of the back shows, however, that instead of the vertical line of stitches at the back of chain, there are instead pairs of horizontal stitches. These appear to have been worked in two journeys, the needle held horizontally, producing a V-shaped stitch on the right side.

(Fig. 10.) The colours are worked in vertical stripes on the background, imitating the hatching of a woven tapestry.

Another Scottish embroidery that employs the same stitch is a large panel, also for the house, probably a table carpet, with the initials *K O* and arms of Oliphant resting on the howdah of an elephant. The initials are those of Katharine Oliphant, who married before 1565, her second husband, George Dundas, seventeenth laird of Dundas and first of Arniston, Midlothian. There are two oval medallions. (Fig. 11.) One shows an aged Paul, with wine glass in hand and flagon at his feet, urging Timothy to take a glass of wine: 'PAVL SAYING TO TEMOTHE THK A LYTL VYN TO COMFORT THY STOMORK'; in the other a gentleman with flat cap and wearing a gown with slashed sleeves gives loaves to a tattered beggar: 'THE LORD COMMANDS THE TO BREAK YE BREAD AND GYE YT YE HOVNGRY'.

Two other sets of valances are related to the Campbell of Glenorchy panels. One came from Balhousie Castle, Perth, which before 1600 belonged to the Earl of Gowrie, head of the Ruthven family. These, like the Campbell set, show the story of Adam and Eve, but drawn in greater detail. The figures in the six incidents depicted are all taken from small woodcuts in *Quadrins historiques de la Bible*, published in 1553 in Lyons by Jean de Tourmes, and illustrated by Bernard Salomon (1508–61). The other valance is a single strip (fig. 12), and bears the arms and initials of Sir Colin Campbell of Glenorchy, grandson of Katherine Ruthven, and his wife, Julian Campbell of Loudon, Ayrshire. This can be dated to the nine years between 1631 when Sir Colin succeeded his father, and 1640 when he died. Worked in tent stitch in coloured wools and unbleached linen thread, it consists of compartments containing heraldic animals at the base of flowering trees: the pink, the strawberry and heartsease. Both these valances are in the Metropolitan Museum, New York.[6]

Related to the Campbell strip valance, a remarkable set of eleven small panels, each five inches wide and fourteen deep, has recently been acquired

9. Woodcut from an early printed book:
Supplementum Chronicarum *by Jacobus Philippus
Foresti Bergomensis, published in Venice 1486. This
is not the source of the embroidered design, but
shows a similar iconography, especially the serpent
with the human face. (The British Library IB.22311).*

by the Royal Museum of Scotland. They are
worked on green and yellow shot silk backed with
linen, and display flower motifs echoing those on
the tent stitch valance: strawberry, heartsease and
pink, with lettering above and below. Each panel
appears to have been separated by a plain space.
Together they read: '[SI] R COLINE CAMPBELL OF
G K' and 'DAME IELIANE CAMPBELL 1632'. (Colour
plate II.)

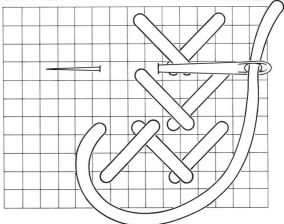

*10. Sketch showing the stitch used on the valances
and on the Arniston panel.*

The ground material suggests that these pieces were part of the bed described in the Balloch inventory of 1640:

Ane silk bed of changing taffite greine and yellow, conteinng iiii piece of curtaines, quhairof iii of Spanische taffite and ane of cesnat [sarsenet] taffite, with ane pand [Fr. *pente:* valance] schewit [sewed] with silk and worsitt with the Laird and Lady Glenvrquy thair names and airmes thairon, with ane greine silk fass [Fr. *fasce:* a horizontal band in heraldry] conteining ii piece, with ane covering wrought with blew and yellow silk.[7]

This finely worked strip on well preserved silk is clearly not the 'pand' sewed with silk and worsted.

---

11. Detail from the Arniston panel, perhaps a table carpet, bearing the arms and initials of Katherine Oliphant, who married George Dundas of Arniston before 1565. 'PAUL SAYING TO TEMOTHE THK A LYTL VYN TO COMFORT THY STOMORK' (I Timothy: 23). Coloured silk and wool on canvas. The stitch is the same as that found on the Campbell valances (fig. 6). The full panel measures 213.4 × 91 cm/83¾ × 36 in. (Mrs A. Dundas-Bekker of Arniston)

12. Two panels of a long valance bearing the arms and initials of Sir Colin Campbell of Glenorchy and his wife, Dame Julian Campbell. He was the grandson of Katherine Ruthven (see fig. 6). He succeeded in 1631 and died in 1640. Silk and wool cross stitch on canvas. Valance measures 40.6 × 309.8 cm/16 × 124 in. (The Metropolitan Museum, New York)

This is rather a description of the valance showing the arms and initials of Sir Colin and Dame Julian, now in the Metropolitan Museum, worked in worsted and linen, not silk thread. To the clerk making the inventory, the white highlights of the linen thread may well have looked like silk. However, the finely worked silk strip, decorated with similar flowers to the valance, could certainly be the green silk 'fass' or band, perhaps serving as an inner valance, or decorating the tester of the bed, thus escaping the inevitable fading and wear that the curtains and bedcover would have received.

The panels of the tent stitch valance, moreover, are bolder, with heraldic animals standing at the foot of each tree. The griffin standing at the foot of a strawberry tree is reminiscent of the motif on the Linlithgow hanging. (See fig. 4.) Another set of this 'tree' design, now stitched together as a single panel, came from Kilbryde Castle, Perthshire.[8] On this, the tree, with animal crouching at its foot, is enclosed in a strapwork frame, embellished with fruit and flowers. The whole piece is drawn and worked with great professional assurance. Until 1643, Kilbryde Castle belonged to the Earls of Menteith. The fourth Earl, John, accompanied the child Mary, Queen of Scots to France in 1550, so the valances may have been acquired in France. These valances also have some connection with the Campbell valances. In 1587, the 6th Earl of Menteith married Mary Campbell, daughter of Sir Colin and Katherine Ruthven. Yet another set, of unknown provenance, but probably Scottish, is in the Royal Museum of Scotland. In addition to the tree motif, this shows fashionably dressed figures depicting the Five Senses.[9]

This set links the 'tree' design with what is the largest and most complicated group of valances: those that show figures wearing fashionable French costume of the late sixteenth century.

Because of this, they have become linked with the name of Mary, Queen of Scots. No valances of this type can be found in the inventories of her reign. Only in the inventory of 1578, made after the Queen had left Scotland, together with the frames of the dismantled embroidery workroom, was there 'a pand of cammes drawn upon paper and begun to sew in silk' (a canvas valance drawn out on paper, and begun to be sewn in silk). In Scottish inventories a distinction was made between *sewn*, embroidered, usually in tent stitch on canvas, and *broidered*, indicating appliqué work.

The costume on these handsome valances, especially that worn by men, consists of French fashions of the type worn after Mary left France, during the reigns of her husband's brothers, Charles IX and Henry III. It is probable, therefore, that these valances were made during the early years of the reign of Mary's son, before he succeeded Elizabeth to become James I of Great Britain. Nor are the valances exclusively Scottish, but may also be found in France, England and Germany. It must be regarded as a European fashion in furnishing, adopted by the wealthier

13. *Valance:* Daniel Rescued from the Lions' Den. *Nebuchadnezzar, carrying a sceptre, and members of his retinue, dressed in fashionable French court costume, watch Daniel being hauled up on a rope,* *while his accusers are thrown to the lions below. Coloured wools and silks in tent stitch on canvas. 56 × 105 cm/22 × 50 in. (The Duke of Buccleuch and Queensberry)*

Videns Rex Danielem a Deo Ifraelis inter leones feruatum, extrahi iubet.

Scottish families, drawn out and worked in professional workshops. There is as yet no evidence as to the location of these workshops.

One striking set, belonging to Lord Forbes, shows the story of Diana. The valances have been stitched together to make a rectangular hanging. Inexplicably, the lowest valance is that belonging to another set, now in the Royal Museum of Scotland, Edinburgh.[10] This set belonged to the Earls of Morton, descended from Sir William Douglas of Lochleven. The lowest valance on this hanging is undoubtedly from the story of Diana belonging to Lord Forbes.

14. Engraving: Daniel Rescued from the Lions' Den *(Daniel VI: 23–4) by H. Cock after Martin Heemskerck, 1565. 19.5 × 24.5 cm/7½ × 9½ ins. (University of Glasgow, Stirling Maxwell Collection)*

A single valance belonging to the Duke of Buccleuch offers valuable evidence as to how these panels were drawn on to the canvas. Since the depiction of the human figure offered the greatest difficulty to pattern drawers for embroidery, engravings and woodcuts were freely used, with the costume altered, perhaps following fashion plates. The valance shows a crowded scene (fig.

Qui Danieli periculum crearant in foueam conijciuntur, protinusq̃ deuorantur .

15. Engraving: Daniel's Accusers are Flung to the Lions. *Published by H. Cock after Martin Heemskerck, Antwerp 1565.* (University of Glasgow, Stirling Maxwell Collection)

13). In the centre is the figure of Daniel being hauled up on a rope from the lions' den (Daniel VI: 23–4). (Fig. 14.) Beside him, one of his accusers is already being eaten by a lion. The richly dressed Nebuchadnezzar, sceptre in hand, is attended by the ladies and gentlemen of his court, the men wearing ruffs and earrings. The figures of Daniel, and of his accuser, are taken from two engravings

published by H. Cock in Antwerp in 1565.[11] (Fig. 15.) This is no amateur piece, and could only have been drawn and worked by a professional, with a collection of engravings to hand.

Even more detailed and assured is a large hanging at Scone Palace, long ago attributed to Mary, Queen of Scots. This is richly allegorical, showing the female figures of Justice and Peace embracing, from Psalm 85, with a border illustrating scenes of Divine Justice from the Old Testament, such as Jezebel being devoured by dogs, and of Peace: the wolf lying down with the lamb. The whole panel, including the border, derives closely from an engraving by Jean Wierix published in Antwerp around 1574, six years after Mary had left Scotland for ever.[11]

References

1. *Accounts of the Lord High Treasurer of Scotland* vol. 11, p. 204.
2. Ibid., p. 362.
3. Ibid., p. 430.
4. T. Thomson, *Collection of Inventories of the Royal Wardrobe and Jewelhouse*, 1815, p. 238.
5. SRO GD16/32/1/562, Airlie Papers.
6. E. Standen, 'Two Scottish embroideries in the Metropolitan Museum', *Connoisseur* vol. CXXXIX, 1957, p. 196.
7. G. Innes (ed.), *The Black Book of Taymouth*, Bannatyne Club, Edinburgh, 1855, p. 349.
8. In the collection of Mr Eric J. Ivory.
9. Royal Museum of Scotland no. 1959.584.
10. Royal Museum of Scotland, acquired 1973.
11. M. Swain, 'Engravings and Needlework of the Sixteenth Century', *Burlington Magazine*, May 1977, p. 343.

CHAPTER THREE

Mary, Queen of Scots

Today, four hundred years after her execution, Mary, Queen of Scots still arouses passionate interest and controversy. Books, plays and operas have been written about her stormy life and tragic end. To some, she was a Catholic martyr, the blameless victim of a spiteful rival; to others, an adulteress who connived at the murder of her second husband. Her reputation as a needle-woman, however, remains unquestioned, for a large number of pieces bearing her initials and her personal cipher may still be seen at Oxburgh Hall, Norfolk, at Hardwick Hall, Derbyshire, and at the palace of Holyroodhouse in Edinburgh.

She became Queen in 1542 when she was six days old, the only surviving child of James V of Scotland and his French wife, Marie de Guise. The English king, Henry VIII, conducting an intermit-tent war with Scotland, proposed that the infant Queen be sent to England, to be brought up to be the bride of his son Edward, thus uniting the two kingdoms. Instead, at the age of five, she was sent to the French court as the intended wife of the Dauphin, the eldest son of Henry II. She married the Dauphin at the age of fifteen. The following year her young husband succeeded his father as François II, and she became Queen of France. A year later, in 1560, her mother, the Regent, died in Scotland, the Scots parliament established the Reformed religion, and in December her husband, the young king, died. (See figs. 16 and 16a.)

Mary returned to Scotland in 1561, a tall, good-looking and vivacious girl of eighteen, well edu-cated and musical, but ill equipped to rule her turbulent kingdom, torn by the dissension of its contentious nobles. The English envoy wrote to

Queen Elizabeth soon after her arrival: 'I was sent for unto the Council Chamber, where she herself ordinarily sitteth the most part of the time, sowing at some work or another' – an astonishing sight to him, for his own Queen did not deign to sit in on the deliberations of her Council.

The Scottish Queen led an energetic life during the next seven years, and must have had little time for needlework. She hunted, rode to the north, visited her castles in Stirling, Linlithgow, Falkland and Lochleven. She married Henry Darnley and rode with him on the 'Chaseabout Raid', when her rebellious lords fled over the border to England. She bore a son, the future James I of Great Britain. Darnley was murdered, and within three months she had married James Bothwell, widely believed to be his murderer. A month later she was imprisoned by her nobles in the island castle of Lochleven, where she remained under close secur-ity for ten months, only to escape to a longer captivity in England.

It has been widely believed that she spent her time on Lochleven placidly embroidering, and several large pieces are attributed to her needle during this period. This belief has its foundation in a phrase from a letter sent by the English envoy to Queen Elizabeth dated 18 July 1567[1] noting her request for 'an imbroderer to draw forth such worke as she would be occupied about'. This is frequently quoted without considering its wider

16. Mary, Queen of Scots, at the time of her marriage in 1558 to Francis, the Dauphin of France. Engraving by Pieter van der Heyden. (Scottish National Portrait Gallery)

REGINA ✠ MARIA IACOBI SCOTORVM REGIS FILIA SCOTORVMQVE NVNC

P.
Æ.

33

Votre tres humble et tres obeisßante fille

Marie

context. Mary had been taken suddenly by night to Lochleven, more or less in the clothes she stood up in, with one, or at most, two of her women. Elizabeth heard with alarm the Scots' treatment of their anointed Queen. Her envoy in Edinburgh, Sir Nicholas Throckmorton, who was not allowed to visit Mary, wrote that he had seen a letter from her to her lords, requesting that, if she could not be set at liberty, at least she might be moved to Stirling Castle, to be near her child. If she were obliged to remain on Lochleven, she asked for one of her gentlewomen, an apothecary, 'some modest minister' (a priest), an embroiderer, and a *valet de chambre*. These requests were not granted, though one of her gentlewomen was permitted later. Her embroiderer, Pierre Oudry, and Servais de Condé were both devoted personal servants, whose loyalty to her was unquestioned, and who would have certainly aided her in any attempt to escape.

When she did finally escape after ten months, she fled to England to seek the aid of Queen Elizabeth. Instead, she entered into a captivity that ended only with her death. As next in line to the English throne, Mary could not be allowed to appear at court, to become the focus for all the dissident Catholics in the kingdom. Instead, she was put into the reluctant custody of the Earl of Shrewsbury, in Sheffield and his other castles in the centre of England, away from London, and away also from the Scottish border. At last, she had all too much time to embroider. 'All day', she told a visiting envoy, 'she wrought with her needle . . . the diversity of the colours made the work less tedious, and [she] continued till very pain did make her give over.'

At first, while she was still on good terms with Shrewsbury's wife Elizabeth, the redoubtable Bess of Hardwick, they 'devised works' together, discussing designs for small panels of canvas work, easily worked in coloured silks on a portable rectangular frame. The designs, often birds and animals, flowers and vegetables, were chosen from the woodcuts of printed books of natural history. There were also emblems, those curious small cartoons illustrating a Latin motto, totally obscure

17. Octagon. One of the panels applied to the so-called Marian Hanging at Oxburgh Hall, Norfolk. Cross stitch in coloured silks on canvas. The central monogram reading MARIE STVART is flanked by thistles and surmounted by a royal crown. To the right of the panel is Mary's personal cipher engraved on her signet ring; in the border the motto Sa vertu matire, an anagram on her name. (Victoria & Albert Museum. Crown copyright. On loan to Oxburgh Hall, Norfolk)

18. *The central panel of the Marian Hanging. A hand with a pruning knife cuts out the unfruitful branches of a vine, with the motto* Virescit Vulnere Virtus. *The Queen's cipher is beside the left trunk. A cushion bearing this design was sent by the Queen to the Duke of Norfolk before his execution in 1572. (*Victoria & Albert Museum. Crown copyright. On loan to Oxburgh Hall, Norfolk)

19. *A Cruciform panel applied to the green velvet Marian hanging:* DELPHIN *(dolphin). Cross stitch in coloured silks on canvas. Below the dolphin, the initials* MR *appear beneath a royal crown. Some of the silks have perished, exposing the bare canvas. The design is taken from a treatise on the dolphin by Pierre Belon, published in Paris in 1551. (*Victoria & Albert Museum. Crown copyright. On loan to Oxburgh Hall, Norfolk)

Ne fault eſtimer, cõbien que lon peigne le Daulphin courbe, ainſi que la figure ci apres propoſee te mon-
ſtre, que la uerité en ſoit telle: mais cela a eſté inueté par les anciens peintres & ſtatuaires, pour monſtrer
le principal & plus admirable acte du Daulphin, qui eſt, que quand la tempeſte doibt uenir ſur la mer,
il fait de grãds ſaults iuſques a paſſer quelquesfois par deſſus un nauire, & enſaultãt, ſemble courbe ainſi
que lon uoit un baſton iecté en l'air, faire un demi cercle en rondeur. Mais a la uerité, il ne ſe courbe pas
ainſi en l'eau, & n'eſt la nature d'aucun poiſſon nager en ceſte ſorte.

20. Woodcut: The Dolphin, *from Pierre Belon's* La Nature et Diversité des Poissons, *Paris 1555.* (National Library of Scotland, Edinburgh)

to us today, but which the educated man or woman of Mary's day recognized and enjoyed solving. These canvas work panels were drawn out, on an enlarged or reduced scale, by an embroiderer. Lady Shrewsbury employed several, whose wages were the cause of a squabble between the Earl and herself. The drawn designs, outlined in black silk cross stitch, were then completed by the Queen, by Lady Shrewsbury, or one of their ladies. Fortunately for posterity, Mary had the admirable habit of embroidering her initials or the cipher engraved on her signet ring[2] on to some of the pieces. (Fig. 17.)

In 1584 Mary was removed from Shrewsbury's custody, and confined more closely. In June 1585

an inventory was made of all her belongings, and a list made of her servants with a view to reducing their number. One was Charles Plouvart, an embroiderer. The inventory includes a large number of embroideries. There were unfinished bed hangings 'wrought with needlework of silk, silver and gold, with divers devices and arms, not thoroughly finished', that were, on her death, to be delivered to her son, the King of Scots.[3] Amongst other pieces, many unfinished, were 52 different flowers in *petit point*, some cut, some uncut, 124 birds, 116 others, 16 four-footed beasts and 52 fish.

It is from this store that the panels mounted on green velvet hangings at Oxburgh Hall, Norfolk,[4] are believed to have come. After four hundred years, the silks are remarkably undimmed, but the designs are meaningless without some knowledge of Mary's life. There is, for instance, the rectangular centrepiece bearing her cipher and the arms of

21. Cruciform panel: A PHESANT, with MR in pale yellow below the bird's head. Cross stitch in coloured silks on canvas. (Victoria & Albert Museum. Crown copyright. On loan to Oxburgh Hall, Norfolk)

Scotland. In the centre a hand with curved pruning knife cuts out the unfruitful branch of a vine (fig. 18) with the motto *Virescit Vulnere Virtus* ('Virtue flourisheth by wounding'). This design appeared on a cushion sent by Mary to the Duke of Norfolk, with letters, when he was implicated in a plot to kill Elizabeth. The cushion and its message was cited as proof of her complicity. The unfruitful vine, Elizabeth, was to be cut down and the fruitful branch, Mary, would rule in her stead. The plot cost the Duke his life; Mary was temporarily reprieved. (Fig. 18.)

A cruciform panel shows a leaping dolphin

worked in blue silk with the initials *MR* and a royal crown. (Figs 19 and 20.) The design is copied from a woodcut in *La Nature et Diversité des Poissons* by Pierre Belon, a physician who was also a naturalist, published in Paris in 1555 while Mary was at the French court. The design is pleasing, but the needlework is also a visual pun. The French noun *le dauphin* means not only a dolphin, but is also the traditional title of the eldest son of the King of France, whom Mary married in 1558.

Not all the panels bearing the Queen's initials can be so easily understood. The 'Unicorne' and the 'Lyone' are heraldic beasts, though the lion she chose to embroider is not the lion rampant of Scotland. Some of the game birds must have been known to one who had hunted in French and Scottish forests. Even the familiar pheasant was included, although its long tail could not be accommodated in a cruciform panel, so was cut off and laid neatly above. (Figs 21 and 22.)

The Queen did not initial her embroideries in order to convince posterity that they were the work of her hands. It may be that those made in the company of Elizabeth Shrewsbury were so marked in order to prevent them from being acquired by that rapacious lady, intent on furnishing her many houses. The panels are worked mostly in cross stitch, with occasional chain or braid stitch to emphasize lettering or highlight lozenge compartments, as on the Hardwick cushion. She used a singularly limited repertoire of stitches, and like her countrywomen in Scotland, does not appear to have shared the contemporary passion of English needlewomen for intricate composite stitches for their own sake. She had been educated in France, and to the end of her days remained sufficiently French for every piece she undertook to be functional, suitable for some article of dress or furnishing: a cushion or valance, a bed or wall hanging.

References
1. *Illustrations of the Reign of Queen Mary*, Maitland Club, Edinburgh, 1837, p. 220.
2. The ring is now in the British Museum, and bears the letters *MA* superimposed on the Greek letter *Φ*, the initial of her first husband, Francis.
3. This is believed to have been the bed later refurbished when James visited Scotland in 1617. See chapter 4.
4. The needlework hangings, property of the Victoria & Albert Museum, are on loan to Oxburgh Hall, Norfolk, which belongs to the National Trust for England and Wales.

   For the French influence on her needlework, see: P. Wardle, 'The Embroideries of Mary Queen of Scots: Notes on the French background', *Bulletin* of the Needle and Bobbin Club, New York, Vol. 64, nos. 1 and 2, 1981, pp. 3–14.

   For illustrations of all the known pieces of embroidery by Mary, Queen of Scots, see: M. Swain, *The Needlework of Mary, Queen of Scots*, Van Nostrand Reinhold, 1973.

22. *Woodcut:* Pheasant, *in C. Gesner's* Icones Animalium, *Zurich 1560. (*The University of Edinburgh*)*

CHAPTER FOUR

The Professional Embroiderer in the Seventeenth Century

In 1603, on the death of Queen Elizabeth, James VI of Scotland, the only child of Mary, Queen of Scots, left Edinburgh with his family to become James I of Great Britain, thereby exchanging the contentious Scottish nobility and the disapproving Kirk for the liveliness of Shakespeare's London. Many Scottish nobles followed him, anxious not to lose the preferment that only the King could confer, and drawn by the opportunities that the richer capital, so near the Continent, could offer. The departure of the court to London must have caused a drop in orders for the professional embroiderers of Edinburgh who, unlike their counterparts in the Broderers' Company of London, had no church work to undertake, since the Presbyterian church set its face against ornament.

It is reassuring, therefore, to find that even after the King left for London, professional embroiderers were still able to make a living in Edinburgh. The Incorporations (or guilds) of different trades in Edinburgh were strictly maintained to ensure a high standard of workmanship, and jealous of their privileges. There was no separate Incorporation of embroiderers to approximate to the Broderers' Company in London. Instead, they formed part of the Incorporation of Tailors, and it may have been this wider affiliation that enabled so many of them to survive. The Court of Session (law courts) and the Scots parliament meeting in Edinburgh ensured that heraldic work was still required, and embroidered costume, albeit of a sober aspect, still had its place in polite society.

King James visited his northern kingdom only once after 1603. This was in 1617, when he desired, he said, to obey a 'salmonlyke instinct' to return to his native soil. For a period of twelve weeks he stayed in Scotland, bringing with him a vast train of luggage, for which relays of cart horses had to be provided from one point to the next. He stayed only briefly in Edinburgh, preferring to hunt and hawk in the country. Hasty efforts had to be made to refurbish the palace of Holyroodhouse, left forlorn after 1603. The Scottish Privy Council ordered four beds to be renovated for his arrival.[1] The hangings were to be sent to London 'thair to be mendit and provided with furniture answerable and suitable to the beddis, and thairafter returnit and send home with diligence'. Three were embroidered: one with scenes of the labours of Hercules, another 'incomplete, sewit be his Majesties mother of gold, silver and silk' appears to have been the one described in detail by William Drummond of Hawthornden in a letter to Ben Jonson dated 1 July 1619,[2] decorated with emblems and *impresas*.

A hanging of green velvet 'embroiderit with holaye leavis in gold with the airmes of Longaveill' was in such poor condition that it was ordered to be given to Nicolas Elesmere to patch it up with several other pieces of green velvet lying in the Wardrobe. He was probably an upholsterer rather than an embroiderer.[3] On the eve of the King's departure from London, an urgent message was received from him ordering 'his Majesties robe royall be sent to his Majestie with all convenient haist, to the effect that his Majestie may provyde himself of ane new robe after the fassion of the auld, yf so be his Majestie shall find the auld one to be so worne as sall not be fit to be carryed by his Majestie in ony grite solemnitie'. By the time the

23. *Royal arms of James VI of Scotland and I of Great Britain, possibly made for his visit to Scotland in 1617. Heavily padded silk appliqué with silk and metal thread embroidery. As well as the Garter motto* Honi soit qui mal y pense, *there is at the base* Beati sunt pacifici *('Blessed are the peacemakers') one of the King's favourite mottoes. The arms are mounted on a board. 160 × 122.5 cm/62 × 48 in.* (Trustees of the Royal Museum of Scotland RHB8)

order was received, the King had already left London on his progress north. It seems improbable that the thrifty monarch saw fit to replace his Scottish 'robe royall'.[4]

The King's Embroiderer in Scotland, William Betoun (or Beatoun) was still in Edinburgh. He had not followed his royal master to London as the Broderers' Company would have effectively pre-

vented him from working there. Possibly he was responsible for the panel bearing the royal arms of James VI, thought to have been made for the King's visit, bearing one of his favourite mottoes *Beati sunt pacifici* ('Blessed are the peacemakers'). (Figs. 23 and 24.) William Betoun lived till July 1620. His daughter Elspeth, married to Robert Bruce, a saddler, was the executrix of his estate which included a debt of £553 6s. 8d. owed to him by the late Earl Marischal, perhaps for heraldic work undertaken.[5]

The names are known of other professional embroiderers working in Edinburgh. A family named White (Quhyte) consisted of James,

24. *Detail of fig. 23. The crowned unicorn is to the left of the arms, in the Scottish fashion, and supports the saltire, the cross of St Andrew.*

43

they signed the National Covenant in 1638 as a protest against the Prayer Book and bishops that Charles I attempted to impose on the Presbyterian church. One, Alexander Barnes, who became burgess in 1633, owned land for which he paid feu-duties (ground rent).[6] The other, Hew Tod, lived till 1671. He had no children and died after a long illness, with sums owing to him from the Incorporation of the Hammermen (metalworkers, including cutlers and goldsmiths) and the Tailors, to which he himself belonged.[7] His widow, Janet Cunningham, survived him by ten years and appears to have been left in comfortable circum-stances, for she was able to make generous bequests to relatives.[8] Both these embroiderers lived in the Canongate, near the palace of Holyroodhouse, as did Adam Gordon, embroid-erer, who married Bessie Gib on 14 July 1640 and became burgess in September 1656. Thomas Forrester, embroiderer, who became burgess in the Canongate in August 1632, is recorded as serving in the watch that policed the burgh, and was named its overseer in October 1645. There was also Robert Porteus, who was given an order for the Royal Arms for the Session House (High Court) in 1661.

What kind of embroidery did all these professionals produce in their workshops? Few documented pieces have survived to show their skill. In the absence of direct evidence, heraldic embroidery of high quality that remains is often ascribed to London, rather than Edinburgh. This seems unnecessarily cautious, for the in-corporations of Edinburgh, like the guilds of London, demanded a high degree of competence in the work commissioned. One piece, a mantle of the Order of the Thistle, is undoubtedly Scottish, for it has no English counterpart.

In 1687, James II (James VII of Scotland) brother of King Charles II, revived the ancient Scottish

broudstar (1613), William, his eldest son (1620) and another son, also called James. They were all embroiderers, and all became burgesses and were therefore allowed to carry on business in the city. Two embroiderers so described themselves when

26. *Mantle of the Order of the Thistle: Gold thistles embroidered on green velvet, with an embroidered silver shoulder badge of St Andrew. (See colour plate III.) Worn by James Drummond, 4th Earl of Perth, when the Order was revived by James II in May 1687. The eight knights created on that day all became Jacobites, and the Earl of Perth followed his master into exile. Queen Anne reconstituted the Order in 1703, when a plain green velvet mantle with shoulder badge was ordained. (The Grimsthorpe and Drummond Castle Trust)*

Order of the Thistle, whose early origins are unknown. He created eight knights of the Order: the habits, laid down by statute, included 'a mantle or robe of green velvet, lined with white taffeta, with tassels of gold and green, the whole robe parsemée or powdered with thistles of gold embroidered, upon the left shoulder of which, in a field of blue, St Andrew his image, bearing before him the cross of his martyrdom in silver embroidery'. A portrait by Kneller of one of the knights, John Drummond, Earl of Melfort, shows him wearing the regalia (fig. 25), and even more remarkable, the complete outfit belonging to his brother James, Duke of Perth, has survived (fig. 26 and colour plate III), showing heraldic embroidery of high quality. The Order was revived by Queen Anne in 1703, when the plain green mantle with shoulder badge, as now worn, was substituted. The robes of all English orders of chivalry are plain: the handsome Thistle robe reflects that of the French Order of St Esprit (1579), powdered with tongues of flame, symbol of the Holy Spirit.

Of the eight knights of the Order of the Thistle created by James II, all, with two doubtful exceptions, became Jacobites. Four followed their royal master into exile in 1688 when he was forced to relinquish the throne. He was succeeded by the Dutch William III and his wife Mary, who brought in their train Scottish exiles of the opposite persuasion, Protestant and Whig, and restored them to favour. One was Sir Patrick Hume, who became Earl of Marchmont (1641–1724). He had spent many years in exile in Holland; his son had served in William's personal bodyguard there. Sir Patrick Hume was appointed Lord Chancellor of Scotland in 1696. He wrote to his son: 'At Whit Sunday '96 when the King made me his Chancellor, I was obliged to borrow money, not being suitably provided of furniture and equipage for my station,

27. *Lord Chancellor of Scotland's Purse, to be carried before him on ceremonial occasions, such as the Riding of Parliament. It belonged to Sir Patrick Hume, 1st Earl of Marchmont, appointed Chancellor by William III in 1696. Padded silk and metal embroidery on velvet. It shows the royal arms in the Scottish fashion with the unicorn supporter on the left. 46 × 49 cm/18 × 19 in.* (The Royal Ontario Museum 968.5/a)

and getting nothing of my salary till the Martinmas [11 November] thereafter.' The Purse (fig. 27), the receptacle of the Great Seal, was symbolic of the office of the Chancellor. It was carried before him on all occasions connected with the Scottish parliament.[9] The Purse, now in the Royal Ontario Museum, differs in many respects from those made for the English Lord Chancellors. Apart from the

28. Standard of Andrew, 3rd Lord Rollo, a supporter of William III, who raised a troop of horse that encamped outside Dundee in 1689. Coloured silk embroidery on cream silk. The corner monograms stand for Andrew, Lord Rollo. (Lord Rollo)

thistles, the supporting unicorn is on the left in the Scottish fashion, not on the right, and carries a saltire. The Scottish badge of St Andrew with its motto *Nemo me impune lacessit* is imposed on the motto of the House of Orange, *Je Maintiendra*. On the death of King William in 1702, Lord Marchmont was 'overwhelmed with grief' and was permitted by Queen Anne to retain his office for a while. His daughter Grisell, who had shared his exile in Holland, married George Baillie of Jerviswood. They were later to buy the estate of Mellerstain in Berwickshire. Her detailed accounts, often with trenchant comments, provide a vivid picture of household expenditure in Scotland during the first half of the eighteenth century.

In 1689 ten troops of horse were raised in Perthshire and the surrounding counties. The silk standard of Lord Rollo's troop still survives. It is of white silk on a linen foundation, and displays a horseman wearing armour, with the motto *La Fortune pase partout*, and the elegant monogram *ALR* (Andrew, Lord Rollo) in each corner in couched silk cord. The troop of forty-six men was encamped outside Dundee in 1689. (Fig. 28.) It may be assumed that the other troops carried equally handsome distinguishing standards. One displaying the well-drawn arms of Spalding of Ashintully and Glenkiln, another Perthshire family, may have been made for the same occasion. (Fig. 29.).

Even after the turn of the century, heraldic work, especially anything requiring silver or gold, was still being commissioned. In 1726 James, fifth Earl of Wemyss, was appointed Lieutenant General of the Company of Archers. He forthwith ordered a complete outfit, the bill for which still exists, as does the uniform itself. Moreover, a portrait of the Earl wearing it hangs in the Archers' Hall, Edinburgh. (Fig. 30.) The outfit included a velvet bonnet:

JAMES CUMING

To 1 blew Velvett Bonnett	£0 14 0
To 1 embroidered St. Andrew	0 7 6
To 2¼ yds silver and green ribbon	
at 2/2	0 4 10½
To 1¼ Richest Open silver lace	
at 12/−	0 15 0
To 9½ Drop silver fringe at 9/−	0 5 4
	£2 6 8½

29. *The Spalding Banner. Cream silk with the embroidered arms of Spalding of Ashintully and Glenkiln in Perthshire. This may have been carried at the same time as that of Lord Rollo. (Trustees of the Royal Museum of Scotland LF15)*

30. *Portrait:* James, 5th Earl of Wemyss *wearing the*
outfit, still surviving, that he ordered in 1726 on
being appointed Lieutenant General of the Company
of Archers.

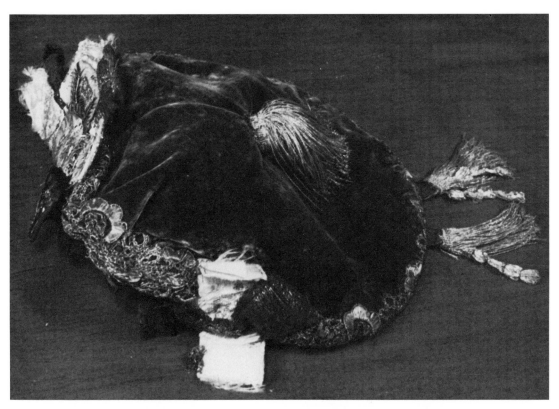

31. *Bonnet of blue velvet trimmed with silver lace and silver and green ribbon worn by James, Earl of Wemyss in his portrait. The bonnet cost £2 6s. 8½ d.* (Lady Victoria Wemyss)

James Cuming was the tailor who supplied it all, but as we know that embroiderers were included in the Incorporation of Tailors, he may well have been responsible for the silver badge of St Andrew that is part of the bonnet. (Fig. 31.)

These surviving examples suggest the type of work undertaken in the workshops of the professional embroiderers in Scotland. (Figs. 32 and 33.) Even in London, members of the Broderers' Company fell on hard times during the Commonwealth (1649–60), when the Court was in exile and Cromwell imposed unadorned Presbyterian worship upon the Church of England. We now know that during that time professional embroiderers drew out designs for domestic needlewomen.[10] This must have been so in Scotland also. Many of the domestic pieces of the period are too well drawn to be the work of an amateur, even when the stitchery shows a high degree of competence. The domestic needlewoman was often capable of superlative technique, but she found it difficult or impossible to achieve good figure drawing, for instance. The example of Mary, Queen of Scots shows how heavily the domestic needlewoman, even the most skilled, relied upon the expert to draw out her designs on to the fabric.

32. *Engraving:* The procession of the Riding to Parliament, Edinburgh, *before 1707 (detail). Embroidered horse trappings and ceremonial cushions were made by professional embroiderers. The rider carries the ancient Crown of Scotland.* (Trustees of the Royal Museum of Scotland)

33. Tabard of a Herald of the Lyon King of Arms, bearing the arms of Scotland as used between 1707 and 1714. Satin ground with silver and silver-gilt metal thread embroidery and gilt spangles. Worn on ceremonial occasions, heraldic embroidery continued to be made in Scotland after the Union of the two parliaments. (Trustees of the Royal Museum of Scotland 1888–303)

References

1. *Register of the Privy Council of Scotland* vol. X, 1613–16, p. 625.
2. See M. Swain *Historical Needlework*, Barrie and Jenkins, 1970, p. 114–16, where it is printed in full. It is not known what became of this bed. The Hercules bed appears to have been taken to London after the King's visit, for one is listed at Hampton Court in 1659, docketed 'this bed taken out of Scotland'.
3. *Register of the Privy Council of Scotland* vol. XI, p. 37. This hanging, bearing the arms of the first husband of Marie de Guise, mother of Mary, Queen of Scots, must have been brought from France in 1538, so it is not surprising that it was shabby.
4. *Register of the Privy Council of Scotland* vol. XI, 18 March 1617.
5. SRO CC8/8/52. For a scholarly description of the embroidered arms, see A. Henshall and S. Maxwell, 'Two seventeenth century embroidered Royal Coats of Arms' *Proceedings of the Society of Antiquaries of Scotland* vol. XCV, 1961, pp. 284–90.
6. M. Wood, (ed.) *Book of the Records of the Ancient Privileges of the Canongate*, Scottish Record Society, 1955. Charter of Confirmation 5 Aug. 1652.
7. SRO CC8/8/74.
8. SRO CC8/8/76.
9. The Lord Chancellor's Purse, originally the receptacle of the Great Seal, was carried before him on all State occasions. It is still carried before the Lord Chancellor at the Opening of Parliament in Westminster. It is now used as the receptacle for the Queen's Speech.
10. J.L. Nevinson, 'John Nelham's Needlework Panel', in the *Bulletin* of the Needle and Bobbin Club, New York vol. 65, Nos 1 and 2, p. 17, 1982.

CHAPTER FIVE

The Domestic Needlewoman
in the Seventeenth Century

In seventeenth-century Scotland, needlework was by no means the elegant pastime of ladies with leisured hours to fill. Indeed, the supervision of a large household, punctuated by successive pregnancies with the resulting large family, left little time for leisure, especially when children's health and education needed daily care. All household linen had to be cut, hemmed and made up into tablecloths, napkins, sheets and 'pillowberes', as well as shifts and shirts. Textile furnishings such as cushions, bedhangings and chair covers could be ordered, but most were made at home, particularly in remote districts. Husbands and friends were often commissioned to bring back materials, designs and clothing, often to their confusion when what they brought back was unacceptable. In November 1669, Katherine Hume wrote to her husband, the Laird of Kimmerhame:

My dearest,

I am in such confusion at your staying so long from me that I know not what to wret bot to obey you and let you hear we are al wel, only I want my dear's pleasant conversation which is beter to me nor health ore any other thing in this world.

Tibi . . . is wel pleased with her bodies [bodices] and I as ele [ill]. I have sent mine back again for they are so stret [tight] that I cannot wear them, besed [besides] they are so slight that I beleve they would not lest [last] two months, therfor I intret you gar give them back again and get me a per of strong twel [twill] ones if there be ony . . .[1]

It is not surprising that the crestfallen Duke of Hamilton, husband of Duchess Anne, on a similar occasion, wrote to her from London:

I confess I like this trade of buying things worst of any, for I see I do not understand it.

The purchase of material for embroidery required even more discrimination than for clothing. Silks and worsteds could not be ordered as required by post. They had to be amassed for use whenever possible. Agnes Keith, Countess of Morton, died in 1684 in Kirkwall on the island of Orkney, to the north of the Scottish mainland. Her belongings were carefully listed by her maid, Bessie Webb:

Compt of the Wardropy Somtym in the Custody of Besse Webb. Servitour to the most noble Laydy Morton, 11 March 1650
1 Gryt Sweet Bagg soad with pitty point
1 Gryt Sweet Bagg Imbrodered with silber and gold
1 littl Whyt Box with Purling with ane number of other small things therin
3 Sweet Baggs Imbroded with gold and silver of Taffety
1 pound and half of new Collourd Silk
$\frac{1}{2}$ pund of Sowing gold besides old Collours of silk

1 Trunk containing therin
1 Whyt fustan bedd, sow'd with Incarnat worsett whereof 15 pieces in it
4 pieces of Galls great and small
1 little box with ane dosson ells of blak and gold Ribbons therin
1 little Flanders Basket wrought with ane woven

silk Kusshon therin unmead up
1 pund and half new Collord silk
½ pund sowing gold, besyds old cullors of silk
(in another chest)

1 geyt woodin cabinett with Shottles containing therin
½ Book of Gold
½ stone of collord worsett
½ pound of small Naples Silk of all cullers
½ pound Ingramed worsett

Some other sind [?things]
2 Dosson fox skinns
1 Barroll of Blak Woll
1 Extraordinary great Glas in a box of
Sweetwood, showing the half of the Boddy
6 Gryt Bibles
1 Sowing book of all cullors guylded, with gold
on the cover[2]

The Countess of Morton was probably not exceptional in the amount of silk and wool she had stowed away with other small treasures. The sweet bags were for perfumes: dried orris root and lavender, rose petals and other herbs. The oak galls may have been intended for the making of ink. The great Bibles could well have been illustrated, serving as embroidery designs for pictures or hangings. Silvered glass for mirrors had only been introduced into Britain at the beginning of the century; so large a one must indeed have caused amazement in this remote castle in 1650. The 'sowing book of all cullers guylded' is, alas, an unsolved enigma.

Crewel work

The bedhangings of white fustian (linen and cotton in a twill weave) embroidered in crimson wools sound most attractive. The half stone (seven pounds) of coloured wools (crewels) would have been ample for working another set. Judging by the pieces that have survived, these crewel work bedhangings must have been very popular. They were decorative, hardwearing and warm, and as acceptable in the cold New England winters as in the chilly castles of Scotland. In March 1687 a Boston merchant, Samuel Sewell (1652–1730) wrote from Massachusetts to a friend in London:

I have two small daughters who begin to goe to school: my wife would intreat your good Lady to pleasure her so far as to by for her, white fustian drawn, enough for curtains, wallen [valance] counterpaine for a bed and half a doz. chairs, with four-threeded green worsted to work it.[3]

By ordering the fustian with the design drawn out on it, Samuel Sewell was ensuring that his wife had the latest fashionable design from London. To work it all in one colour avoided the danger of running out of a certain shade at so great a distance from the source of supply. The light and dark shades could be achieved by using a wide variety of different stitches.

The earliest known example of crewel work bedhangings to survive in Scotland are the pieces worked on cotton/linen twill that is stamped on the reverse 'Bruges 1640' within a wreath. (Fig. 34.) They belong to the descendants of Sir George Bruce of Culross, who died in 1643. His ships traded with the Netherlands and the Baltic. No records are as yet available about the manufacture of this twilled cloth in Bruges, nor indeed in Britain, though it is the common foundation of the crewel work curtains that survive, so must have been easily available. Although very durable, it sometimes perished with use, and the firmly worked embroidery with its coiling stems and massive leaves was then cut out and re-applied to a new ground, not always happily.

This has befallen an interesting piece from Cullen House, Banffshire, part of a set of bedhangings, the embroidery of which has been remounted on to a shiny satin to make a counterpane for a bed with different curtains, worked later. (Figs. 35 and 36.) The heavy crewel work of the bedcover has a curious base of rocky hillocks in which lurk animals and orientals. This bears elements that appear also in a set of three painted

34. *Fragment of a large bed hanging. Crewel work embroidery on cotton/linen twill that is stamped on the reverse 'Bruges 1640', presumably the mark of the authorities of that city who had passed the cloth for sale. 33 × 40 cm/13 × 15¾ in. (The Earl of Elgin and Kincardine)*

and dyed cotton hangings made for the European market in western India around 1700. This painted set was auctioned at Ashburnham House, Sussex, in 1952, together with four embroidered curtains (figs. 37 and 38) and a palampore of the same design.[4] In addition, there is a coverlet with the same rocky border now in the Royal Ontario Museum, but worked in silk chain stitch, indication of an Indian origin, rather than the European crewel work of the Cullen piece. It is not known how this design came to be in a castle in the north-east of Scotland, nor who worked it.[5]

Crewel work curtains, or fragments from them, are found in many other Scottish country houses, notably Traquair, Naughton, Monymusk and Wemyss Castle. (Fig. 39.) Other crewel work curtains at Cullen were worked by Anne Smith (second wife of Brigadier Grant), who had been a Maid of Honour to Queen Anne. They are more delicate in style than the bedcover just referred to. At Blair Castle a set of crewel work curtains are the work of Helen Dallas of Edinburgh, whose bill is dated 7 May 1753. This is an all-over design of sinuous stems and flowers in polychrome crewels, and is not so solid as the seventeenth-century technique. The remains of another set in the same house shows a powdering of flower sprigs on a cotton/linen foundation.

The fashion for crewel work bed curtains lasted, therefore, for over a century in Scotland, until the middle of the eighteenth century. It has been assumed that by then they had become hopelessly old-fashioned, though little evidence has been

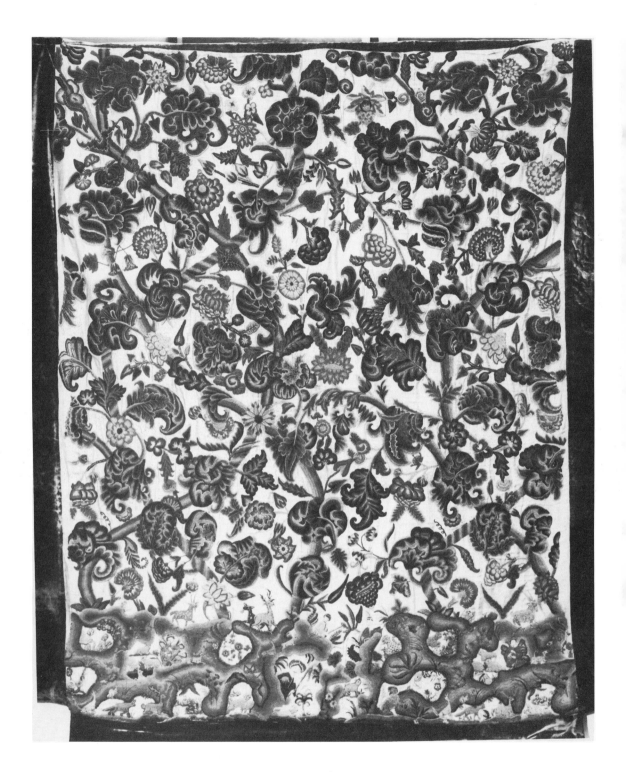

56

35. OPPOSITE *Bed cover, once a bed curtain from Cullen House, Banffshire. Crewel work that has been remounted on to shiny satin. Similar details appear on painted and dyed cotton curtains made in India. (Trustees of the Royal Museum of Scotland)*

36. *Detail of fig. 35, showing figures and animals in a rocky landscape.*

offered to support this. Indeed, the Duchess of Argyll still had a set on a bed in Edinburgh in 1753, as an advertisement makes clear:

Stolen from Her Grace the Duchess of ARGYLL and GREENWICH's house at CAROLINE PARK the CURTAINS OF A BED, being of white FUSTIAN lined with white calico, large Flowers sewed with red and green, but mostly green, and the

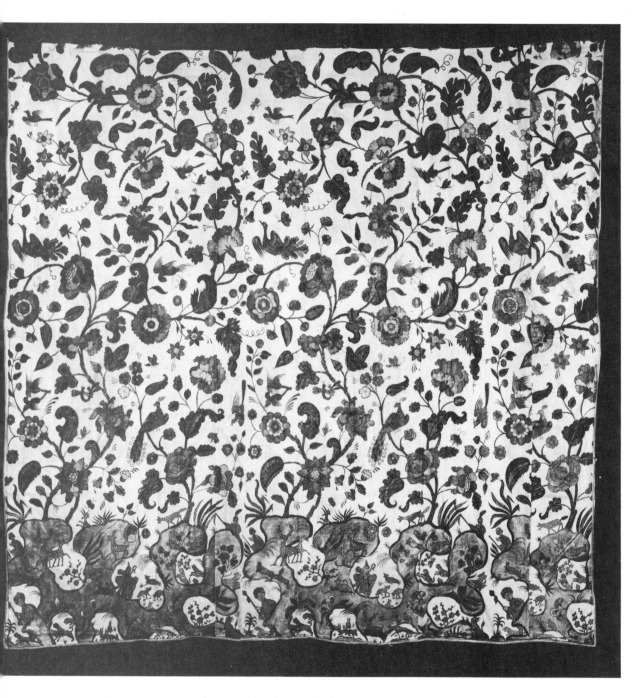

37. Hanging, Gujarat India, painted and resist-dyed glazed cotton made for the English market, 1675–1725. 246 × 257 cm/97 × 101 in. (Museum of Fine Arts, Boston. Samuel P. Avery fund and gift of Mrs Samuel Cabot)

38. Detail, fragment of a bed curtain, crewel work on linen. Compare the figure on the left with a feather in his hat facing the leopard, and the man playing a pipe with mountain goat above, with similar details on the Cullen bedcover (fig. 35). 66 × 104 cm/26 × 41 in. (Museum of Fine Arts, Boston. Elizabeth Day McCormick fund)

roots of the flowers Hair coloured, bordered with green Silk Lace, and a scalloped Bord. round the Foot of the curtain about Half-quarter and Nail broad with red sprigs and small Olive Leaves. In order to discover the Person who stole them, Ronald Dunbar, her Grace's Factor, Writer to the Signet, hereby obliges himself to pay Five Guineas to any person who shall discover who the guilty person is . . .[6]

'Slips'

A more economical and effective way of decorating bed hangings and valances was by working motifs first on canvas in fine tent stitch. These were then cut out, and after pasting at the back to stiffen them, were applied to curtains of linen, wool, silk

39. Crewel work valance from Wemyss Castle. 25.5 × 132 cm/10 × 12½ in. (Lady Victoria Wemyss)

40. *Panel from a set of bed hangings of red velvet, ornamented with applied 'slips' in fine tent stitch on canvas, and applied twist border in the same stitch. Associated with Mary, Queen of Scots. (The Earl of Mansfield)*

or velvet. They could easily be transferred to new material when the old wore out. It is, of course, the method used in mounting the cruciform and octagonal panels worked by Mary, Queen of Scots on to the hangings at Oxburgh Hall, as well as the thistles on the green velvet Thistle Robe. These tent stitch motifs were often called 'slips', since they frequently depict the slips or cuttings used in vegetative propagation of plants illustrated in herbals and other engravings, from which the embroidery designs were copied. A great many of these fine tent stitch motifs survive in Scotland. At Scone Palace bed hangings of red velvet, now faded to a tawny colour, are decorated with slips of

flowers, insects and animals, edged with a Renaissance twisted border. (Figs. 40 and 41.)

'Ane rid skarlett tablecloth, shewed with bouk [animals] and slips' was listed at Tyninghame in June 1635.[7] The Duchess of Hamilton's fine Drawing Room at Hamilton Palace in 1690 contained 'a dozen of kain chairs and a dozen of imbroidered velvet cushions with slips' and a carpet for the floor.[8] Elaborate hangings of blue linen line the walls of King Malcolm's Room at Glamis. They bear handsome tent stitch appliqué of flowers, together with a little crewel work. They are topped by richly fringed pelmets on which can be discerned the date 1683 and HELEN COUNTES OF

---

41. *Detail of another panel of the same set, showing the applied 'slips' and twisted border. The red velvet has faded to a tawny hue. These bed hangings were in use until the 1940s. (The Earl of Mansfield)*

42. *Pelmet of wall hangings around King Malcolm's Room, Glamis Castle. Fine tent stitch motifs applied to blue linen with the arms of Patrick, Earl of Strathmore and Kinghorne. They bear the date 1683.* (The Earl and Countess of Strathmore and Kinghorne)

STRATHMORE & K. and PATRICK EARL OF STRATHMORE AND KINGHORNE. Patrick, third Earl of Kinghorne, was created Earl of Strathmore in 1677. He married Lady Helen Middleton in 1662. (Figs. 42 and 43.)

The richest collection of these slips is undoubtedly that at Traquair in Peeblesshire. There is a quantity of uncut panels, all in mint condition, crammed with flowers, birds and animals, as well as unfinished pieces, and yards of twisted Renaissance border designs all in fine tent stitch of wool and silk. It is not known who worked all these pieces, but the family produced some notable needlewomen. This large store had been packed away unused, so that the bright colours are undimmed. (Fig. 44 and colour plate IV.)

It must have been a similar store that provided

43. *Detail of one of the wall hangings at Glamis Castle. The applied motifs are outlined with fine cord and surface stitching.* (The Earl and Countess of Strathmore and Kinghorne)

mounted on a yellow silk damask to make delicate wall panels for a drawing room after the house was rebuilt in 1702.

the decoration of the handsome Victorian curtains in the dining room of Haddo House, Aberdeenshire, where slips of birds, flowers and animals worked in the seventeenth century have been mounted in the nineteenth century on to heavy purple velvet. (Fig. 45.) At Lennoxlove, now the home of the Duke of Hamilton, slips were

Pictorial panels

Scotland did not escape the fashion for small needlework pictures of Biblical subjects, mostly from the Old Testament, worked by children and young women in the seventeenth century. An engaging pair at Glamis are dated 1679 and 1681

respectively. They show the *Sacrifice of Isaac*, and *Jacob receiving his father's blessing*. They are thought to be the work of children of the family; the drawing as well as the stitchery is very amateur.

At the other end of the scale are the four large needlework pictures now in St Nicholas Kirk, Aberdeen, also depicting Old Testament stories. They show the *Finding of Moses*, *Esther before Ahasuerus*, *Susanna and the Elders*, and *Jephthah's Daughter*. They were bought in 1688 'for the decorment of the King's Loft in St. Nicholas Kirk' by the Town Council of Aberdeen, who paid Baillie George Aedie £400 Scots (about £33 sterling) for them. The *Moses* panel has Aedie's initials and those of his wife, who is believed to have worked them. Mary Jamesone was the daughter of George Jamesone, the artist, and she married George Aedie as her third husband in 1677. She died in 1684.

The panels are six feet high and vary in width from twelve feet six inches to just over seven feet. There was a fifth smaller panel, now lost, which was used as a table cover on which the church plate was laid at Easter and Christmas. It has been suggested[9] that the panels were made to be hung around a room in the manner of woven tapestries, which they strongly resemble, even to the borders; in which case the smallest, *Jacob wrestling with the Angel*, the panel now lost, would have hung over the fireplace. It is remarkable that the panels

45. Close-up of a cockerel applied to Victorian curtains of purple velvet in the Dining Room at Haddo House, Aberdeenshire. The tent stitch motifs on the curtains may have come from a panel such as those at Traquair. (The National Trust for Scotland)

46. *Large wall panel:* The Finding of Moses, *bearing the initials of George Aedie and his wife, Mary Jamesone. They were married in 1677, and she died in 1684. Linen ground, entirely covered by wool embroidery with silk for the flesh and some details. The background is unworked in the borders. 233 × 223 cm/92 × 88 in. (The Kirk Session of St Nicholas Church, Aberdeen)*

should have survived at all, for they have been moved several times when the church (in reality two churches) was rebuilt: one side by James Gibb in 1755, and the other in 1835 and 1875. They had been mounted as a single group on to 'strong old canvas fishing sails' and were rescued, 'wet and smoke-begrimed' after the fire that burnt down the east church and steeple in 1874. They were then cleaned by Pullars of Perth, and placed in the vestibule of Gibbs' West Kirk, where they remain. Around 1880 they were framed and glazed to prevent people from pilfering the threads. (Fig. 46.)

The *Esther* panel derives from an engraving published about 1660 by N. Visscher in Amsterdam, after the design by Martin van Heemskercke. The *Moses* panel must have been worked after 1667, when George Aedie married Mary Jamesone. There seems no reason to doubt that they are the work of Mary Jamesone, since hangings requiring large frames, and even large carpets, continued to be made by the domestic needlewoman in Britain during the succeeding century.

References
1. SRO, Hume of Marchmont papers, GD 158/2720/17.
2. SRO, Morton papers, Box 156, no. 14.
3. 'The Letter Book of Samuel Sewell' Vol. I, 1686–1712, in *Collections of the Massachusetts Historical Society*, 6th Series I (Boston, 1886).
4. J. Irwin and K.B. Brett, 'The *Origins of Chintz*' HMSO, 1970, p. 67.
5. J. Vollmer and I. Krasuski, 'Preserving the past. An Indian embroidered coverlet' *Rotunda*, Summer 1981, Vol. 14, no. 2, pp. 24–31.
6. *The Caledonian Mercury*, 9 August 1753. I am indebted to Vanessa Habib for this reference.
7. W. Fraser, 'Memorials of the Earls of Haddington', Edinburgh, 1889, Vol. II, p. 300, no. 414.
8. Hamilton papers, 126/8/8. I am indebted to the Duke of Hamilton for allowing me to quote from this.
9. W. Kelly, 'Four needlework panels attributed to Mary Jamesone', *Miscellany of the Third Spalding Club* Vol. II, Aberdeen, 1941.

CHAPTER SIX

Domestic Embroidery in the Eighteenth Century

Mary Jamesone's large needlework hangings have survived because they were bought for a church, and have remained there ever since. Had they been left in the Aedie house, demolished around 1914, they would have been discarded long before. The Old Testament heroines would have been too old-fashioned for later taste. Smoke from the domestic fires would have blackened them, and later generations would have replaced them with fresh and fashionable wallpaper. Not all domestic needlework was discarded, however. Indeed, Scotland is fortunate that so many pieces are still to be seen in the houses for which they were made.

An enchanting set of four bed curtains is still in use at Wemyss Castle. Dated 1727, 1728, 1729 and 1730 respectively, they were worked by Janet, daughter and heiress of Colonel Francis Charteris. In 1720 she married James, fifth Earl of Wemyss, the owner of the bonnet and uniform worn as Lieutenant General of the Company of Archers. (See fig. 30.) The bed curtains, which are very long, are worked on fine linen woven with a broad pale-blue satin stripe, with pots of delicate flowers and chinoiserie birds embroidered at intervals in coloured silks. Although the outlines are repeated, the flowers are worked in different colours on each motif, so that a lively variety is achieved. (See colour plate V.) As each curtain was made, the Countess added the initials of herself and her husband, and those of her children as they were born, as well as the date. These are hidden on one of the vases. The initials are tiny: less than a centimetre high, and worked in fawn silk, so that a search must be made to find the initialed vase on each curtain. (Figs. 47a and b.) It is sad to record

that the Countess and her husband became estranged soon afterwards, and she left her family (and the bed curtains) behind to live unhappily till 1778.

Chair covers

More surprisingly, since they are subject to even greater wear than bed hangings, well-documented chair covers still grace the houses for which they were made. They have no doubt survived because, in the eighteenth century, upholstered chairs were almost invariably provided with 'cases' or slip covers of linen or checked cotton, only removed on important occasions. Indeed, sometimes they were not even removed when the owner sat on a chair for a portrait. There is a delightful painting at Lotherton Hall, Yorkshire, of an unknown lady sitting at a table knotting, while her husband regards her fondly. She is seated on a high-backed upholstered armchair with a slip cover of green check.

At Blair Castle, Perthshire, a set of eight striking mahogany chairs are to be seen, upholstered in canvas work. On the back and seat of each chair is a cornucopia filled with flowers, the flowers different on each chair, glowing in vivid colours against a dark brown background. They are said to

47. *Close-up of a pot of flowers on a bed curtain at Wemyss Castle, with the date 1729 and initials. (See key, fig. 47a; and colour plate V.) (Lady Victoria Wemyss)*

47a. *Key to fig. 47.*

| DAVID LORD ELCHO b.1721 | HON. JAMES WEMYSS b.1726 | | LADY WALPOLE b.1724 | LADY HELEN b.1729 |

E F I F W A H

| | FRANCIS LATER 6TH EARL b.1723 | LADY FRANCES b.1722 | LADY ANN b.1727 | |

IW

JANET
COUNTESS OF WEMYSS

W

JAMES
5TH EARL OF WEMYSS

be the work of Jean Drummond, second wife of the second Duke of Atholl, whom she married in 1749. They are obviously amateur work: the stitchery is slightly uneven, and the design on the back is set too high, as if insufficient canvas had been allowed at the top. In a professionally worked piece this would not occur. (Fig. 48.) The account for the chairs shows that the handsome frames were made in London to receive the covers. They were made by William Gordon, whose bill, dated 17 June 1756, for eight mahogany chairs with fish-scale carving, includes the item: 'To making an addition to your Grace's needlework £2. 5. 0.' This was possibly the filling in with brown worsted of the ground at the front of the seat, to accommodate the curved edge. The set of chairs cost £31.

The bill for a later set of twelve chairs and two settees with bolster cushions may still be seen at Blair Castle. This set, in the Drawing Room, also had the frames made to receive the needlework covers, believed to have been made by Charlotte, daughter and heiress of the second Duke by his first wife. Charlotte married her cousin, John Murray of Strowan, who succeeded as third Duke. She had seven sons and four daughters. She died in 1805. The chairs and settees were ordered from Chipchase and Lambert, London. The cost of the first chair, a sample, was £3 3s., to which was added: 'To white worsted and making out the ground of the needlework, 8/-'. The sample chair was painted white, but apparently not approved, as the set, delivered in 1783, had gilded frames. Twelve chairs and two settees cost £103 11s. The ground of the canvas work was white, now faded to a silvery cream, and shows flowers in a beribboned medallion of oak leaves, worked in long and short stitch. More than one person must have worked the set: some of the chairs have a cross stitch ground, others tent stitch (half cross stitch).

A piece that can confidently be attributed to Duchess Charlotte is a pole screen made from broomwood, an unusual wood employed by a Perth cabinet maker to make several small pieces for Charlotte's father. The needlework panel is now rather worn, as the black yarn has perished. It is in tent stitch and bears the date 1759 and the initials *JMC*, for John and Charlotte Murray. They were married in 1753, and he succeeded her father as third Duke in 1764.

Other needlework covers include a floral drop-in seat dated 1750, and some so-called 'country chairs' with covers of a characteristic geometrical design in four shades of blue worsted, worked in rice stitch, using graduated shades to make a striking trellis design. Rice stitch ('crossed corners') used in this way in a counted design reminiscent of Florentine patterns appears to have been popular in Scotland during the second half of the eighteenth century. Understandably so, since the design is counted out like a knitted pattern, and no drawing is required. Moreover, rice stitch, a cross stitch with crossed corners, is very hardwearing. There is a handsome set of six chairs in this technique at Drum Castle, Aberdeenshire, (fig. 49), and an armchair at Mellerstain that is depicted in a portrait of 1828. Curiously, the only other cover of this type outside Scotland has been encountered in Philadelphia, attributed to Elizabeth Coates Pascall (1702–67). It is worked in rice stitch in a typical 'flame stitch' or Florentine pattern of overlapping carnation heads.[1]

A handsome mahogany settee at the palace of Holyroodhouse, Edinburgh, belongs to a set comprising a pair of smaller settees and six side chairs, all covered with canvas work depicting classical and other scenes on the backs with floral medallions on the seats. (Fig. 50.) They belonged to Lord Adam Gordon (1726–1801) who, as Commander in Chief of North Britain, was granted an apartment on two floors of the palace in 1782. This he proceeded to furnish in some style, as he had married, late in life, Jean Drummond, dowager Duchess of Atholl, whose eight chair covers are still at Blair Castle. (See fig. 48.)

---

48. Mahogany chair with fish-scale carving, made by William Gordon for the second Duke of Atholl, 1756. Covers of silk and wool on canvas. The frames were made to receive the covers. (The Duke of Atholl)

In 1796 Lord Adam chivalrously loaned his apartment and furniture to the Comte d'Artois, exiled heir apparent to the French throne and later Charles X of France, while the State apartments of the palace were being prepared for occupation by the Bourbon prince. Lord Adam died in 1801, when his apartment was still occupied, and the furniture passed to the Crown. The chairs and small settee covers at Holyrood had, understandably, become worn and shabby over the years, and

50. Mahogany settee with needlework cover at the Palace of Holyroodhouse. One of a set of two smaller settees and six side chairs that once belonged to General Lord Adam Gordon. Fine tent stitch on canvas. (By gracious permission of Her Majesty the Queen)

in 1920, when HM Queen Mary undertook the refurbishing of the palace, some of the ladies of Scotland made new canvas work covers, copied from the old, to renew the chairs and make them worthy of a royal palace. These were presented at Buckingham Palace before being mounted on the chairs. One of the needlewomen, Lady Rose Leveson-Gower, who was abroad, was represented by her younger sister, Lady Elizabeth

49. Mahogany chair, one of a set of six, covers worked in rice stitch in graduated shades of yellow and green. At Drum Castle, Aberdeenshire. (The National Trust for Scotland)

Bowes-Lyon, who was to marry Queen Mary's son and become the Queen of King George VI.

Much of Lord Adam's furniture was inherited from his mother, Henrietta, Duchess of Gordon, who had bequeathed to him her house and its contents at Prestonhall, Midlothian. It is now known that the set of seat furniture came from her, rather than his wife. The Duchess of Gordon was a remarkable woman. The widow of the second Duke, a member of a devout Catholic family, she received a pension from the Hanoverian government for bringing up her twelve children in the Protestant religion. This was forfeited, however, when she impulsively laid out breakfast for Prince Charles Edward Stuart as he passed her gates on his way south in 1745. Indeed, Lord Adam's career as a professional soldier was retarded for some years by the suspicion of Jacobite sympathies. (Fig. 51.)

His mother's other activities may have obscured her reputation as a needlewoman, though the Gordon papers reveal that she was ordering embroidery material in London in 1752. An account of Edward Vaughan, haberdasher of small wares, at the Old Royal Point, corner of St Michael's Alley, Cornhill, London, advertised:

Great choice of the best and newest Fashion Patterns for Ladies' Work Viz^t Brussels, French Quilting, Cross Stitch, etc. with great variety of shades in Silks & Worsteds. Likewise Canvas & Callicoes, plain and Figured Dimitys, Muslins, Lawns & Cambricks with all materials for any sort of Needle Work.

The Duchess of Gordon bought, among other things:

July, French Crap[e] & stick [stitch] worsted   12/-

Dec.6.White worsted	12/-
Drawing of 2 Jars and a Bason	3/-
Drawing of 2 Sprigs	1/-
Drawing of the Vall^c & Bas	6/-

Chair covers at Chatsworth are embroidered with a design of oriental jars and teapots. The last entry probably refers to a valance and base (lower valance) for a bed.

There is, moreover, a finely worked firescreen at Gosford bearing her initials and the date 1754. (Fig. 52.) It shows the unusual scene of the risen Christ appearing to his disciples. Other needlework still at Holyrood that belonged to Lord Adam Gordon includes a firescreen showing the *Sacrifice of Isaac* (colour plate VI), and a card table with canvas work top, which displays a three-handed card game, such as Ombre, laid out, with a purse of counters.

Wall panels

Canvas work was not confined to seat covers in the eighteenth century. Its durable qualities were still appreciated for other pieces of household decoration. A large wall hanging in the House of Monymusk, Aberdeenshire, is worked in fine tent stitch on canvas. (Fig. 53.) It shows an arcaded terrace with vases of flowers and a tree standing on black and white tiles against a yellow wall. This large summery panel is dated 1750 and was worked by Anne Grant, daughter of Sir Francis Grant, Lord Cullen, and sister of Sir Archibald Grant, a noted agricultural reformer. It is not known where Anne Grant found her design, though it must have been drawn out for her professionally. There is, however, some indication among the Grant family papers that it may have been an artist living in Aberdeen. A printed notice has been preserved, advertising:

MR. COLLIE Limner
Begs leave to acquaint the Public that he draws PORTRAITS from life in China-ink on

52. *Firescreen:* The Risen Christ at the Tomb with Peter, John and Mary Magdalene *(John XX: 1–12). With initials HG and date 1754. The initials are those of Henrietta, Duchess of Gordon, whose daughter Catherine married the Earl of Wemyss in 1745. Silk and wool on canvas. Very fine tent stitch with cross stitch border. 108 × 81.5 cm/ 42½ × 32 in.* (The Earl of Wemyss and March, KT, LLD)

53. *Wall hanging signed and dated 'Anne Grant 1750'. An arcaded terrace with vases of flowers and a tree standing on black and white tiles against a yellow background. Wool and silk on canvas. Fine tent stitch. 182.9 × 240 cm/ 71¾ × 94½ in.* (Sir Archibald Grant of Monymusk)

paper for 4s, on vellum for 5s. He draws in proper colours on paper or vellum, according to the manner they are done from 7s6d to a guinea. With chalks on paper for 7s6d. With crayons for 7s6d to a guinea; on canvas in oil colours from a guinea to five guineas; without desiring them to sit above a quarter of an hour, or half an hour at most.

He likewise teaches at reasonable rates ladies and gentlemen to DRAW in water colours etc. drawing of human figures, from the first principles to a finished piece; flowers from nature on vellum, silk or paper; landskips and

54. *Sketch showing elevation of a room by Robert Adam, c.1790. Now known to be that of the Drawing Room at Newliston, with two needlework panels indicated. (Sir John Soane's Museum, London)*

55. *Needlework panel, woollen appliqué highlighted with water colour, on a ground of yellow moreen. Once in the Drawing Room at Newliston, this panel was sold in 1928. Its present whereabouts are unknown. (See fig. 54.)*

56. *The Drawing Room, Newliston, today, with
some of the appliqué panels worked by Lady Mary
Hog in place. (*Mr and Mrs J.S. Findlay)

perspective; ornaments such as rock, shells, foliages etc.

He draws and invents flowers or running figures for patterns for sewing chair-bottoms, bed twilts, fire-screens, etc.

He lodges at Mrs. Stewart's in Robert Mitchell's Close, Exchequer-row, Aberdeen.[2]

There is no difficulty in recognizing the style of the designer of some unusual needlework wall hangings in the Drawing Room at Newliston, West Lothian. The house was designed by Robert Adam for Thomas Hog and his wife, Lady Mary, daughter of the seventh Duke of Lauderdale. Originally, there were fourteen panels. Two were taken down when alterations were made to the house. The remaining twelve hung until 1928, when they were taken down, begrimed with the dust from a nearby shale mine, and sold at Sothebys. They then disappeared, until eight came on the market in 1981, and were bought back by the present owners, to occupy, after an absence of fifty years, their original places on the walls. A sketch in Sir John Soane's Museum shows the elevation of one side of the Newliston Drawing Room (fig. 54) with the largest panel in place. This panel was sold in 1928 and is still unlocated. (Fig. 55.)

Robert Adam died in 1792, before the house was quite finished. Lady Mary died in 1795. There is no record of Adam using needlework panels on the walls of any other house: it must be assumed that they were the suggestion of Lady Mary herself, and that she had already embarked on the series before the house was built. The technique was rapid, but extremely effective. The shapes are cut out of material that looks like felt, but is a woven woollen fabric with a nap, perhaps broadcloth, and applied to a ground of moreen, a ribbed woollen material much used for upholstery. The appliqué is held down with widely spaced stitches of tailor's silk, and touched up with water colour. In 1785 Lady Mary had drawing lessons from David Allen, the artist (1744–96). He may have helped with the design of some of the panels.[3] (Figs 56 and 57.)

In addition to the drawing room panels, there is a bed from Newliston in the same technique now on loan to the Georgian House, Edinburgh. (Colour plate VII.) The design is simpler than the wall panels, but no less effective. Ribbon swags decorated with pink flowers and green leaves border the curtains, valances and lower valances. One curtain has been utilized to make a bedcover. The bedroom in which it stood at Newliston originally had window curtains to match. The flower petals and leaf shapes would have been cut out from a template: they are all the same shape, and are held down on the pale yellow moreen of the background by silk stitches widely spaced. The material could have come from tailors' clippings.

This surprisingly modern technique is found also on a fragment at Wemyss Castle. It appears to have been part of a window pelmet. The background is firm grey broadcloth; the applied flowers, of various colours in similar materials, are highlighted and modelled, not with watercolour, as at Newliston, but with fine stitchery in silk. (Fig. 58.) Three small framed and glazed panels of the same period are known: one is at Mellerstain, one at Arniston, and a third, known to have been made in 1790 by Elizabeth, wife of James Whiting Yorke, is now at Wemyss Castle. The design shows a basket of flowers: auriculas, passion flowers and moss roses. In each panel the flowers and basket are identical, even the butterfly. Only the arrangement is different.

Needlework decoration made by the family graced other houses in Scotland, though no doubt much more has been discarded or lost. The Countess of Mar, sister of Lady Mary Wortley Montagu (1689–1762), made a carpet and a screen. The four-leaved screen, with panels of feathers and pots of flowers (fig. 59a and b), is now on loan to the Royal Museum of Scotland. In Castle Fraser, Aberdeenshire, there are on display, in the Sewed Room, bed hangings and seat covers, together with a window pelmet, attributed to Miss Elyza Frazer (1734–1814). They too are worked on moreen, with a delicate floral design in surface stitches, using fine crewels. Haddo House, Aberdeenshire,

57. Portrait: Lady Mary Hog. *Oil on canvas, attributed to David Allan. Lady Mary had drawing lessons from the artist, and he may have assisted in* designing some of the panels. *(Mr and Mrs J.S. Findlay)*

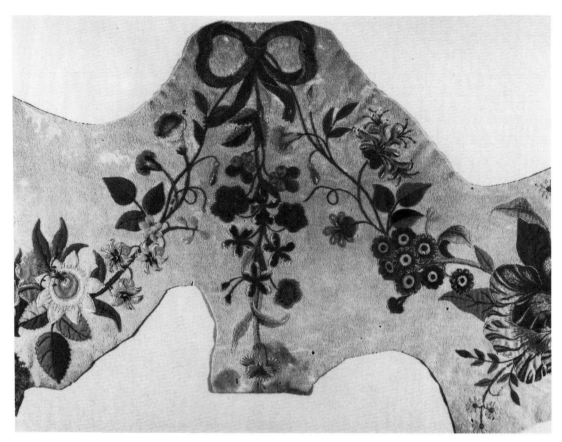

58. Fragment of a pelmet. Coloured wool appliqué on firmly woven dark grey material, with fine silk embroidery details. (Lady Victoria Wemyss)

has handsome curtains, perhaps originally for a bed, worked by the second wife of William, second Earl of Aberdeen. She was Lady Susan Murray whom he married in 1716 and who died in 1725. The daughter of the first Duke of Atholl, she came from a family of notable needlewomen.

Minor needlework

Although a remarkable number of monumental pieces of needlework have survived to this day in Scotland, not all needlewomen undertook the daunting task of bedhangings, or large sets of chair covers. Like their counterparts in England and France, many of them took pleasure in the minor forms of needlework, learning an unaccustomed or fashionable technique to display their skill.

One such technique was learned by the two elder daughters of the fourth Earl of Traquair, who, as members of a Catholic and Jacobite family, were sent to a Paris convent in 1713 to finish their education. Lady Lucy and Lady Anne Stuart, then aged eighteen and seventeen, spent six months at the Ursuline convent of St Jacques. 'There is not a monstray in Paris', wrote Lady Anne to her mother, 'wherein they teach more kinds of needleworks. As for works, we have learned the coly fishes, and to make pursses . . . we have made two pursses, one for my Lord, another for your Ladyship; Sister Lucy has sent hers already, with several things . . . which they do not do in

59. Two panels of a four-leaved screen, worked by
the Countess of Mar, who died 1761. Tent stitch on
canvas. The feathers are worked in surface stitches.
(The Earl of Mar and Kellie, on loan to the Royal
Museum of Scotland)

flowers in flat stitch on both sides of heavy paper [collé fiché] . . . In spite of the neatness of this work, this Embroidery has hardly any usage but to be placed under glass or in books'.[4] (Fig. 60.)

There is a small bookmark in the same technique in a manuscript book of prayers and meditations, now in the National Library of Scotland.[5] Begun in 1743, the volume belonged to Janet Oliphant (1721–58), daughter of Laurence Oliphant of Gask, exiled after the 1745 rebellion. His wife and family shared the privations of his exile in France. Janet, without dowry, married, at the age of thirty-seven, William Macgregor of Balhaldie, another exiled Jacobite, considerably older than she was. Touchingly, the book contains at the end a prayer against miscarriage. Her only child was born in October 1758. She died six weeks later, bequeathing the book to her infant son. The little embroidered bookmark, 9.5 by 7 cm, shows the *Agnus Dei*, the Lamb of God, in white silk with black spots and pink ears. It is exceedingly amateur, compared with the assured pieces at Traquair.

A fashionable pursuit was knotting, which required very little technical skill. We learn much about it in the letters of Mrs Delany, who continued knotting till the end of her long life, after she could no longer see to embroider. Regularly

Scotland.' The 'coly fishes' (French: *colifichet*) were worked in an exacting technique. Four pieces still remain at Traquair. They are finely embroidered pictures worked in floss silks on paper, alike on both sides. Two are flower pieces, two are religious: the monstrance and Host on an altar, in which metal thread is used, as well as silk. This type of embroidery was certainly not one that 'they do in Scotland', for it was mainly practised by nuns in continental convents. 'Some religious communities embroider shaded baskets and bouquets of

MATILDA LOCKHART
SPOUSE TO
GENERAL JAMES LOCKHART
of CARNWATH S.ᵈ
2ᵈ Daughter to
Jnᵒ Lockhart of Caſtlehil
1769

spaced knots were made on a continuous thread of flax or cotton, which was then stitched in a decorative pattern on to bed hangings or clothing. Mrs Delany decorated a set of chair covers with knotting, or 'string work', as it was sometimes called. A portrait of Matilda, wife of General James Lockhart of Carnwath (fig. 61) shows her with workbag and knotting shuttle, the latter with more open ends than the modern tatting shuttle. Similar knotting shuttles were widely used during the second half of the eighteenth century, and many elegant ones survive, some made of gold or silver. Mrs Delany wrote in 1770 of the 'nonpareil shuttle . . . that has claimed les entrées into the best of company', but knotting could also be worked with a netting needle, similar to the ones used for centuries by fishermen for mending nets. It may have been such an implement that Lady Henrietta Johnstone bought in 1698 when she recorded the purchase of a 'noting needle' for four pence.[6] She became the wife of the first Earl of Hopetoun. On the other hand, knotted net, made with the same long needle, could be darned to make a geometrical lace (lacis). Mary, Queen of Scots had asked for such needles to be sent to her while imprisoned on the island of Lochleven. And a later Countess of Hopetoun, Jane Oliphant, wife of the second Earl, chose to be painted at her netting, using just such a needle, for her portrait by Gainsborough. (Fig. 62.) John, second Earl of Hopetoun (1704–81) had three wives, and all of them appear to have been dedicated needlewomen. His third wife, Lady Elizabeth Leslie, had her portrait painted by Gainsborough (fig. 63), and she is shown seated with a circular tambour frame on a stand, tambour hook in hand, and a square of white muslin stretched on the frame. The Earl's first wife, Lady Anne Ogilvie, died in 1759. She evidently

---

62. Portrait: Jane Oliphant, *second wife of the second Earl of Hopetoun, who died in 1767. Oil on canvas, by Thomas Gainsborough. She is shown netting. The corner of the net is attached to a table clamp, and she holds a netting needle in her left hand.* (The Trustees of the Hopetoun Preservation Trust.)

undertook canvas work, for a bill survives, headed 'Lady Hop[t] worsets 1758'.[7] The bill, which has a printed heading, is from:

Thomas Hill, Son in law and Successor to the late Mr. Norman at the Old Adam and Eve, in Newgate Street, against St. Martins le Grand, London, advertises that he sells all Sorts of Worsteds and fine Criule, in Shades, Flos Silks, Canvas for Cross Stitch and Tent Stitch, Patterns drawn on Canvas for Chairs, Screens, Carpets, Curious wrought Patterns, Worsted and Silk Laces and Fringes for Beds, Coaches and Liverys, Knitting Worsted Yarn.

On the back is an account for 17/6 for dark-coloured and white worsted, crimson worsted and crimson silk.

Personal embroidery

Not all embroidery was done for the house. Clothing in Calvinist Scotland tended to be sober, and when the wealthy required embroidered suits or dresses for a wedding or other festivity, they were supplied by tailors and worked professionally. Some were bought abroad, in Paris, Lyons or London, for the Scots travelled and sent their sons to foreign universities in the eighteenth century as in the seventeenth. Snowy linen at neck and wrists showed up all the better against a sombre background, as the Calvinist Dutch had found. But lace had to be imported into Scotland. There were attempts to set up lace schools to encourage this desirable craft, but none were successful. The beautiful Duchess of Hamilton established one in the vicinity of Hamilton Palace in the 1760s, but the lace produced was coarse, and dismissed as 'mere Hamilton'. In Edinburgh and Montrose other schools were set up to teach the craft to orphans, but without success. The chief difficulty was that fine flaxen thread had to be imported and was therefore expensive and the supply unreliable.

However, tolerable ruffles for caps, shirts, shifts and sleeves could be embroidered in imitation of

lace on fine linen cambric or cotton muslin. A shirt ruffle, said to have been worn by Prince Charles Edward Stuart, who led the ill-fated Jacobite forces against the Hanoverian George II in 1745, is now in the Royal Museum of Scotland. It is Dresden work (French: *dentelle de Saxe*), a type of white embroidery originating in Saxony, and widely taught in the many schools for young ladies that were opening in Scotland, as elsewhere, in the eighteenth century. The technique, a repertoire of stitches that pulled together the threads of loosely woven sheer fabric into a variety of patterns, was easy to learn, but the final result, as with bobbin lace, relied on the excellence or otherwise of the design chosen. As always, superlative technique could be marred by a poorly drawn, amateur design.

In one house at least, Balcarres in Fife, this difficulty was overcome by the ingenuity of the governess, who was herself a talented artist. She was Henrietta Cumming, sister of an artist, James Cumming, who became Herald Painter to the office of the Lord Lyon. They may have been related to the James Cuming who supplied the Archer's uniform to the Earl of Wemyss. She also had a cousin, Helen Dallas, who undertook embroidery for John Schaw, a fashionable upholsterer in Edinburgh. Helen Dallas worked the hangings for a bed that Schaw supplied to the Duke of Atholl in 1753, for which she was paid £36.[8] With this background, Henrietta found no difficulty in producing pleasing patterns for needlework. She was also ambitious, with a character worthy of the pen of Thackeray, whose Becky Sharp she very much resembled.

James, fifth Earl of Balcarres, had resigned from the army when he succeeded his brother. He was then in his late fifties, and promptly married Anne, daughter of Sir Robert Dalrymple, and many years younger than himself. They had three daughters and eight sons in rapid succession. The eldest, Lady Anne Lindsay, was born in 1750. She was talented and witty, author of the ballad *Auld Robin Gray*. Her sister, Margaret, was equally talented and vivacious, and both girls early took their places in Edinburgh society, then entering its most brilliant period. Judges, philosophers and writers, including Sir Walter Scott, visited Balcarres. Lord Balcarres died in 1768, leaving a comparatively young widow to bring up her large and high-spirited family as frugally as possible, with a wide circle of family and friends to entertain.

She had found Henrietta Cumming in Edinburgh 'weeping and painting butterflies in the garret of a house where she lodged', wrote Anne later; 'she wept because she was not placed (she said) in the sphere of life for which she was formed'. Installed at Balcarres, she refused to accept a salary and ate with the family, making every use of the social contacts provided, and persuading Lord Balcarres to secure for her a Government pension. She was a voluminous correspondent, with a romantic flight of fancy.[9]

While she was governess at Balcarres, she drew out needlework designs for the young ladies and their mother, and encouraged the boys in the schoolroom to do so too. She drew out designs for others as well, including Mrs Cockburn (Alison Rutherford, 1712–94), the poetess, who wrote asking for a pattern for a ruffle:

Draw me a bold stroke for a pr. ruffles only the edge ther'of – not much show and little work & I care not if it be fruits and birds instead of flowers.

No pieces actually worked by Henrietta Cumming have survived, but three inked designs are signed by her. One, in three pieces, for a cap crown and lappet (*barbe*) or streamer is inscribed in her hand 'This is the lapet and cap which I think vastly pretty.' (Fig. 64.) Other designs are signed by

63. *Lady Elizabeth Leslie, third wife of the second Earl of Hopetoun. Oil on canvas, by Thomas Gainsborough. She is seated at a tambour frame, and the white material is stretched over the circular top, held by a strap; the tambour hook, which made a continuous chain stitch, is held in her right hand. (Private collection).*

64. *Sketch, ink on paper. Design for the lower part of a lappet, or barbe, for a cap. Drawn by Henrietta Cumming, governess to the family of the fifth Earl of Balcarres. On the reverse she has written 'This is the lapet and cap which I think vastly pretty.' About 1761. 22 × 8.5 cm/8½ × 3½ in. (Mary, Countess of Crawford and Balcarres)*

Anne and Margaret Lindsay. (Fig. 65.) Because of their fragility, the lappets and ruffles have no doubt perished in laundering. Not all the lappets, however, were embroidered. In 1766 Henrietta wrote to her sister-in-law, the wife of the Herald Painter:

The Lady Bal. begs you would tell her what kind of bones is fit to make the everlasting white for painting gauze as she is determined her young ladies shall wear no other lappets but of their own painting with the painted Suits. She proposes to have the bones gathered for you here that you may have the less trouble in making.

She chaperoned the girls on their visits to Edinburgh, and became increasingly indispensible to Lady Balcarres, especially after Lord Balcarres died. Henrietta introduced to Balcarres Sir Alexander Fordyce, with whose sister she had been at school. He was a financier, a self-made man with political ambitions, who found in Lady Margaret's ancient lineage and good looks a highly desirable wife. His suit was supported strongly by Henrietta, and Margaret was married to him in 1770 at the age of eighteen. She was installed in his mansion at Roehampton. Meanwhile, Henrietta had been corresponding ardently with his elder brother, the Revd James Fordyce DD, a preacher much admired by George III. In 1771 the minister married Henrietta, who thus became Margaret's sister-in-

65. *Corner design by Lady Margaret Lindsay. On the reverse side is a message in pencil: 'Have you the musick in your care still?' About 1761. 96 × 82.5 cm/ 37¾ × 32½ in. (Mary, Countess of Crawford and Balcarres)*

90

law. The same year, the financier crashed, absconded and caused many bankruptcies as well as heartbreak to his young wife who was left alone. He died in 1789, when Margaret was able to marry again. Henrietta continued to flourish, first as the wife, then as the widow of a fashionable and highly respected divine. She died at Bath at the age of 89.[10]

References

1. Philadelphia Museum of Art. Bequest of Lydia Thompson Morris, 32.45.128.
2. SRO GD 345/1493/6. The printed advertisement is undated, but is docketed 'Feb. 1761. Said to be a Native of Kintore'. Nothing is known of this artist, except a small painting of Mrs Hay inscribed *John Collie* in the Scottish National Portrait Gallery.
3. M. Swain, 'A Georgian Mystery, Lady Mary Hog and the Newliston Needlework' in *Country Life*, 12 Aug. 1982, pp. 470–72.
4. C.G. St. Aubin, *The Art of the Embroiderer*, 1770, ed. E. Maeder, translated N. Scheurer. Los Angeles County Museum of Art, 1983, p. 51.
5. National Library of Scotland MS3197, f. 54.
6. Hopetoun Archives 888, Bundle 398.
7. Hopetoun Archives 888, Bundle 388.
8. F. Bamford, 'The Schaws of Edinburgh and a bed at Blair Castle', *Furniture History*, 1974.
9. The letters are in the University of Edinburgh Library, Laing MS 81.
10. M. Swain, 'A wild kind of imagination', *Country Life*, 26 Jan. 1978, pp. 190–92.

CHAPTER SEVEN

Tambouring and Ayrshire Embroidery

In the autumn of 1782 a professional embroiderer, trained in continental workroom methods, arrived in Edinburgh. His name was Luigi Ruffini, and he came from Piedmont in northern Italy. What brought him so far north is not clear, though Edinburgh was by then a stimulating city, enjoying its most brilliant era. About twenty years before, the more prosperous inhabitants had spilled out of the narrow medieval confines of the ancient town, built along the ridge running from the Castle to the palace of Holyroodhouse. Lawyers and judges, physicians, merchants and country lairds had left the constricting apartments that opened out on to a common stair, shared with their poorer neighbours aloft, and were spreading themselves in the spacious classical streets and crescents of the New Town. The airy houses, with large windows and lofty ceilings, were furnished with mahogany furniture, well made, with an understated elegance.

There seemed to be singularly few openings for a professional embroiderer, however. The interiors of the new houses were hung with window curtains of plain moreen or printed cotton; the walls were painted or stencilled, or else covered with fashionable wallpaper. The national Presbyterian church conducted its services in spartan plainness, without the distraction of decoration or organ music. Roman Catholics, most of whom were still Jacobites, met discreetly in the Cowgate, too straitened in their circumstances to consider ordering opulent vestments. Though there was a little heraldic or military work to undertake, female fashion was changing from the stiff full silk gowns of the first half of the century to plain white muslin,

though warm woollen would seem more suited to the Scottish climate.

Undeterred, Ruffini visited the leading haberdashers with his samples. They referred him to the Board of Trustees for Fisheries and Manufactures in Scotland, for they saw possibilities in the white embroidery that he showed, not hitherto undertaken on a commercial scale in Scotland. The Board of Trustees had been set up after the Union of the two parliaments of England and Scotland in 1707. The Trustees, twenty-one public men and learned judges, administered the sum of £2000 annually to foster the fishing and linen industries of Scotland. As well as subsidizing the fishing industry, they paid premiums for flax sown, paid stampmasters to assess and stamp all linen offered for sale, and set up spinning schools in country districts. They held annual competitions in Edinburgh for the best linen shown. Any money left over was used to encourage new crafts or inventions likely to prove beneficial to Scotland.

Ruffini's application for assistance in setting up his workroom was therefore sympathetically received. The whitework that he proposed to teach his apprentices – Dresden work and tambouring – would enhance the value of any fine linen produced in Scotland, and both, as they knew from their wives and daughters, were in great demand. Dresden work, though popular with amateurs and taught at schools for young ladies, had been produced professionally in Saxony, where men as well as women worked on it. It was for this type of needlework that Henrietta Cumming had drawn out her designs in the schoolroom at Balcarres, but it was exacting work, requiring time and skill to

66. *Corner of a fichu. Drawn muslin, so-called Dresden work: (French: dentelle de Saxe). Believed to have originated in Saxony, this fine whitework consists of lace-like patterns embroidered on sheer muslin or cambric, using geometrical stitches, often pulled together, to give a variety of fillings. Late eighteenth century. (*Trustees of the Royal Museum of Scotland*)

complete. It was in great demand for fichus, caps, and ruffles that could be used on men's shirts as well as sleeves. It made an excellent substitute for lace. The design on the sheer surface of the linen was achieved by a variety of fillings made by pulling the stitches together in patterns. (Fig. 66.) No threads are withdrawn, so that it is stronger than its fragile appearance suggests.

Unfortunately, however, sheer linene was a commodity that could not be produced in Scotland, in spite of all the encouragement of the Board. The flax grown in response to the premiums was suitable for the manufacture of sailcloth, sheeting and even linen damask, but anything finer had to be imported from the Netherlands. The Trustees purchased good flax seed from Riga, which they distributed for planting. In 1729 they had brought over a party of cambric weavers from

St Quentin in Picardy to settle in Edinburgh, hoping that their wives would teach the skill of fine spinning, but this still depended on the supply of fine flax, which was scarce and often impossible to obtain. By 1755 the Trustees noted, 'the manufacture in Edinburgh by foreign weavers has not answered'.

In spite of these difficulties, Ruffini set up his workroom and took on twenty apprentices: young girls under the age of ten, whom he undertook to feed and clothe, following the accepted practice of apprenticeship in Scotland. The children were learning a good clean trade: at this time children were still working underground in the mines of Scotland. It was the century before the Factory Acts began to regulate the hours of children's employment. In 1783 the Trustees took the unprecedented step of paying Ruffini £20, his rent for one year, with the promise that it could be renewed.

The payment of rent was the least of Ruffini's problems: the maintenance of his apprentices, while they learned their trade, was pressing. He replied asking for £80, assuring the Trustees that if they would grant his request, he would have no further need to trouble them. They answered firmly that it would be 'improper to give large sums at once to a manufacture about the success or endurance of which in the country there is any uncertainty', though the Secretary hinted that he might get something further if he deserved it. By June, Ruffini was able to report that he had increased the number of his apprentices to thirty, when the Trustees allowed him a further £30.[1]

In February 1784, when his rent fell due, Ruffini again applied for help. This time it was refused. However, the reputation of his work had spread to the west of Scotland and the cotton manufacturers there began to see possibilities in it, and sent orders. He increased his apprentices to sixty-four, but was continually hampered by lack of capital as well as cramped conditions. In March 1785 he sent a more urgent appeal to the Trustees. He now had no less than seventy young apprentices, whom he 'feeds, cloathes and instructs in his art, but has suffered a considerable loss for some months past

from a slow fever which during that time has confined more than two thirds of them to their beds'. The Trustees sent their Secretary and one of their number, Mr Oliphant, the Lord Provost of Edinburgh, to inspect the premises, which they found altogether too small and ill-ventilated, a fact that Ruffini himself recognized, in an age that was not particularly sensitive to either overcrowding or lack of ventilation. He wished to take more spacious premises recently vacated by a chaise-hirer who had moved to a more fashionable address, in which he could accommodate thirty of his apprentices. To encourage him, the Trustees allowed him £30: £21 for the rent of his new workroom and £9 'for the benefit and accommodation of his apprentices'.

Although sheer linen was almost unobtainable in Scotland, fine cotton muslin was being manufactured in the west. It was a manufacture that owed little to the Board of Trustees, unlike the linen trade. The handloom weavers around Paisley and Renfrew had always been renowned for their fine silks and gauzes; now they were employed in weaving a fine cotton muslin from yarn spun in Scotland's water mills. It was cheaper than the imported Indian muslin, for so long a desirable but expensive fabric. The handloom weavers generally worked for a manufacturer, who supplied the yarn and paid for the finished cloth, which he marketed. The Glasgow manufacturers saw in Ruffini's workshop a way of ornamenting this muslin, using commercial methods in order to enhance its value.

A rapid method of working chain stitch had been introduced from India around 1760[2], using a tambour hook, so named after the circular frame on which the fabric was stretched like the skin of a drum. Tambour work was extensively used in continental workrooms to decorate bed hangings and gentlemen's waistcoats in fine multi-coloured silk chain stitch. Ruffini adapted this technique for white embroidery on the fine cotton muslin, often incorporating the pulled stitches of Dresden work. Instead of the small circular frame, the fabric was stretched over a large rectangular frame, capable of taking almost the full length of the web of

67. *A commercial tambouring frame used in the west of Scotland. The uncut web of material was mounted into the frame with rollers at each end controlled by a ratchet, and the frame was mounted on a table stand. Some of the frames were large enough to accommodate two girls seated side by side, working the designs in a continuous chain stitch on muslin stamped with a water-soluble dye. Wooden roller, length 112.5 cm/44 in., diameter 4.5 cm/1¾ in. (The David Livingstone Museum, Blantyre. Sketch by Don Aldridge)*

muslin, with girls working on either side. The design was printed on to the muslin by means of wooden blocks, using water-soluble dye that could be washed out when finishing. It was this modification that the manufacturers of the west seized upon when they began to set up their own tambour workshops. (Fig. 67.)

Ruffini made another important contribution to the tambour manufacture. He recognized the importance of using trained designers in his workshop, and in 1786 requested that three of his male apprentices be admitted to the School of Design maintained by the Trustees. Set up in 1760 with the express purpose of improving the standard of manufacturing design in Scotland, the School had become rather a drawing academy for artists, but in the year that Ruffini made his request, David Allan had been appointed Master. On the instructions of the Trustees, he endeavoured to restore it to its original purpose, which was to train, in addition to decorative painters and engravers: 'damask weavers, carpet makers, paper makers for

rooms, calico printers, embroiderers, japanners, coach painters and seal cutters'. Students had to be over the age of thirteen, and 'show some proofs of genius for drawing'. Ruffini's apprentices were allowed to stay for three years. Textile designers who trained there provided manufacturers with designs for tambour work, linen damask, printed cottons, shawls and carpets.[3]

Workrooms for tambour embroidery were set up by manufacturers all over the west of Scotland; one, in Renfrew with financial help from the Board of Trustees. Most of them dispensed with the old apprenticeship conditions of feeding and housing the girls. Instead, the girls went daily to the workroom, and once trained, earned from 1/3 to 2/- per week, at a time when a fully skilled weaver earned about 7/- a week. By 1793, when the Statistical Account of Scotland was compiled, the ministers who recorded the details of their parishes mention the tambour manufacture, usually along with muslin weaving. (Fig. 68.) At Paisley, the minister wrote: 'within this twelvemonth many have laid aside the spinning wheel, leaving that useful instrument of domestic industry to be occupied by those of a higher rank, and have applied themselves to the easier, the more elegant, and at present the more profitable employment of flowering muslins'. It was certainly preferable to spinning linen yarn for weavers, the only other paid occupation, apart from domestic service or farm work, then available to country women. Spinning was condemned by the minister of Kirkintilloch because 'some are not a little subject

I. The Fetternear Banner. Coloured silks on fine linen, worked in double running stitch. The centre panel shows the Christ of Pity surrounded by the Instruments of the Passion. Top left are the arms of Gavin Douglas, Bishop of Dunkeld (1515-22) and Provost of St Giles, Edinburgh (1503-22). He was exiled in 1521 and died in 1522, which may account for the incomplete and unused state of the banner. 149.9 x 79.6 cm / 58¾ x 31½ in. (Trustees of the Royal Museum of Scotland)

VII. The Newliston Bed, worked in the same technique as the wall panels (figs 54 and 55), woollen appliqué on yellow moreen. Worked by Lady Mary Hog, who married Thomas Hog of Newliston in 1770 and died in 1795. (Mr and Mrs J. S. Findlay, on loan to The Georgian House, Edinburgh, National Trust for Scotland)

VIII. Sampler signed 'Margret Boog 1761', with the names of her parents, Robert Boog and Margret Orrock. The house, with the man on the steps carrying a staff, appears on other Scottish samplers, but is so far unidentified. Coloured silks on woollen canvas. 32 x 26.5 cm / 12½ x 10½ in.

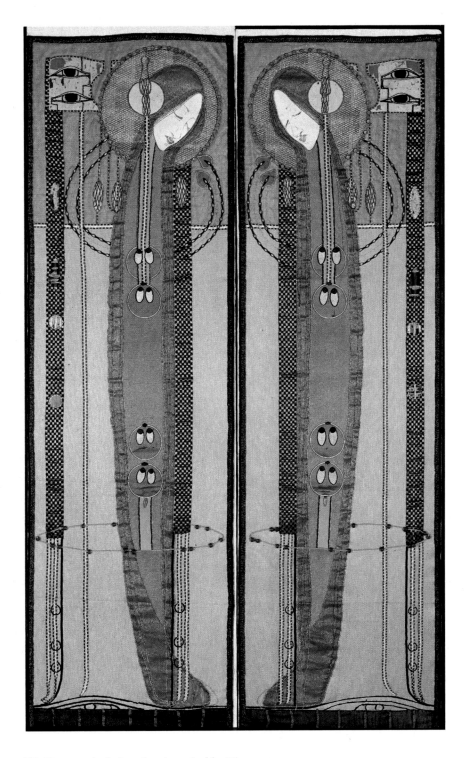

IX. *Two panels designed and worked by Margaret Macdonald (Mrs Charles Rennie Mackintosh, 1865-1933). Braid, ribbon and silk appliqué, embroidered with silk and metal threads on linen and decorated with glass beads. Shown at the Turin Exhibition, 1902. 182.2 x 40 cm / 71¾ x 16 in. (Glasgow School of Art)*

*V. Detail of one of four bed curtains embroidered by
Janet, wife of the fifth Earl of Wemyss, dated 1727,
1728, 1729 and 1730 respectively. On each curtain
she embroidered the initials of her husband and
children. Coloured silk embroidery on fine linen,
woven with a blue satin stripe. (See figs 47 and 47a.)*
(Lady Victoria Wemyss)

VI. Firescreen: The Sacrifice of Isaac. *This firescreen belonged to Lord Adam Gordon, who had a grace-and-favour apartment at the palace of Holyroodhouse. He had inherited the furniture of his mother, Henrietta, Duchess of Gordon. The shape and arrangement of the needlework panel is very similar to one signed and dated 1754 by his mother (see fig. 52). The design is taken from an engraving (VIa) published in Amsterdam about 1660. (By gracious permission of HM the Queen)*

VIa. Engraving: 'The Sacrifice of Isaac', *from* Historia Sacra Veteris et Novi Testamenti, *published by N. Visscher, Amsterdam, about 1660. 40 x 50 cml 15³⁄₄ x 19¹⁄₂ in.*

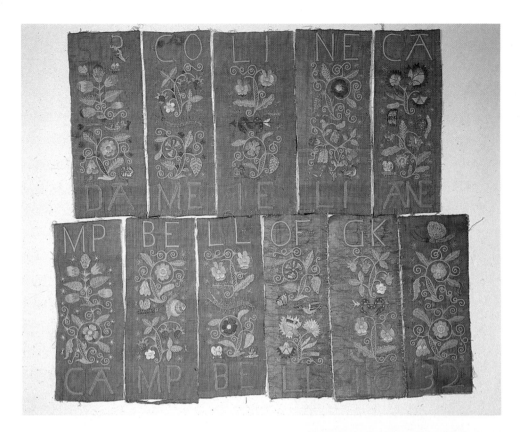

II. Panels of silk embroidery on green and yellow shot silk. Probably the inner lining of the valance of a bed. (See fig 12.) They read: '[SI]R COLINE CAMPBELL OF G K' and 'DAME IELIANE CAMPBELL 1632'. Each panel: 35.5 x 12.7 cm / 14 x 5 in. (Photo: Christies, South Kensington)

III. Shoulder badge of the Thistle Robe (see fig. 26), showing the figure of St Andrew, and motto Nemo me impune lacessit. Professional embroidery of high quality in coloured silks, silver and silver-gilt thread. 18 x 16.8 cm / 7 x 6½ in. (The Grimsthorpe and Drummond Castle Trust)

IV. Detail of another panel of 'slips' at Traquair (see fig. 44). The panels remain uncut and unused, the brilliant colours outlined in black silk. (Mr Peter Maxwell Stuart of Traquair)

X. Frontal for the Communion table, Mayfield
Church of Scotland, Edinburgh. Designed and
worked by Kathleen Whyte. Silk and rayon appliqué
in more than sixty shades, on fawn repp. The Hand of
God, holding the world, is in gold kid. 1972.
(Mayfield Church, Edinburgh)

68. *Detail of a tambour work sampler. From Old Cumnock, Ayrshire, 1800–1810. The designs are numbered for reference, and separated by wavy lines, originally in Turkey red cotton. This shows a swag for a lady's dress, about 24 cm across. The large space has a Dresden work filling, done with needle and thread.* (Trustees of the Royal Museum of Scotland)

---

to hysterics, a disease, the prevalence in this place has, with some show of probability, been attributed partly to the dampness of our earthen floors, and partly to the effects of spinning . . . the women, especially in winter, sit by the fireside, and always keeping the same station, the one side is exposed to the chilling cold of the season, and the other

relaxed by the warm influence of the fire . . . the waste of saliva in wetting the thread must deprive the stomach of a substance essential to its operations, whence all the fatal consequences of crudities and indigestion may be expected'. Cotton yarn, of course, was spun by machinery in mills powered by water.

Not all the ministers approved of the wages earned by the tambour workers: 'Many of the young women flower muslins, by which they not only maintain themselves, but buy fineries,' wrote the minister of Houston and Killallan, while the Revd John Bower, of Old West Monkland, complained that the high wages of the muslin weavers enabled them to marry young, and 'about

200 young girls are employed at dotting, tambouring, etc. Some of them begin at 8 or 9 years of age, and at that early period earn 6d or 8d a day. Although this may be profitable to one class, it is attended by much material inconvenience to another. Farmers complain of the high wages of servants and sometimes have difficulty in procuring them at all. Is there no remedy for this growing evil?'

Unhappily, Ruffini, acknowledged by the Trustees to be 'the first to introduce into Scotland the business of tambouring muslins to the great benefit of the country', did not make his fortune. He had arrived in Edinburgh with high hopes, but lacked capital and a talent for business. His schemes included a plan, when he first arrived, to found a residential academy for boys, teaching French, Italian, writing and arithmetic, with visiting masters for riding, fencing, dancing and military exercise. Nothing was heard of it after the initial advertisement.[4] He married Mary Steel, daughter of John Steel of Jamaica, in 1790, and they had a family. He set up tambour workrooms in Dalkeith and Musselburgh. The last we hear of him is the minute of the Board of Trustees, 8 July 1801, praying for pecuniary assistance to recommence business, 'having been deprived, by unavoidable misfortunes, of the means of supporting his wife and family'. The Trustees refused, on being told that a subscription was being raised by some Glasgow manufacturers.

Ruffini's misfortunes should not be attributed entirely to his fecklessness, for even the tambour workshops in the west suffered heavy fluctuations in trade. During the war with Napoleon, supplies of cotton were intermittent, and although an aggressive businessman like Kirkman Finlay managed to smuggle yarn and piece goods into blockaded Europe, smaller manufacturers saw trade fall away. Handloom weavers and the girls who undertook tambour work inevitably suffered. In addition, fashion changed, and by 1820 the demand for flowered muslins had declined, though tambouring was still carried on in a small way to supply such things as caps and kerchiefs. Within

the next decade, women's dress had changed from the high-waisted muslin gown with its soft folds to a more imposing silhouette with spreading stiff skirt, tiny waist and exaggerated shoulders, topped by a cap decorated with luxuriant loops and frills. Lace was required, or, failing lace, a new type of embroidery.

Fortunately for the Scottish muslin industry, a new type of embroidery was found that could be produced in quantity. A new type of muslin was also required. In place of the soft loose weave a firmer, but still fine, muslin was produced as ground for the new work.

The new embroidery, called 'sewed muslin' to distinguish it from 'tamboured muslin', owed its origin to the energy and enterprise of a woman, Mrs Jamieson. (Fig. 69.) Her husband was a manufacturers' agent living in Ayr. He distributed the cotton yarn to the handloom weavers and collected and paid for the finished cloth. Mrs Jamieson was lent a baby robe embellished with satin stitch and fine point lace insets by Lady Mary Montgomerie, heiress of the Earl of Eglinton, who had married her cousin, an officer serving with the Duke of Wellington. He had been stationed in Naples, where their son, the future thirteenth Earl of Eglinton, was born. The baby robe, said to be French, was brought back to Ayrshire after Lady Mary's husband died in 1814. Mrs Jamieson analysed the lace stitches, taught them to women who would undertake to work them well, and with the help of the muslin manufacturers, established a considerable business. She is said to have controlled a thousand outworkers. Like Ruffini, she appreciated the necessity for professional designers, especially in competition with French whitework. The designs were drawn out in Glasgow, transferred to wooden blocks, and stamped on the muslin using water-soluble blue or pink

69. *Mrs Jamieson, wife of an Ayr cotton agent (one who gave out the spun yarn to handloom weavers and collected the finished webs). She originated the sewed muslin (as distinct from tamboured muslin) industry, later called Ayrshire embroidery.*

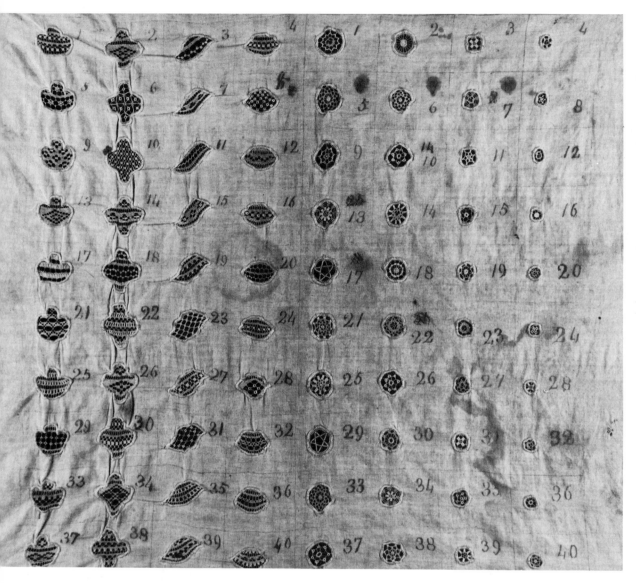

colour. The material and yarn for working was then given to the workers, who had to complete the work at home in a given time, and to an acceptable standard. 'Only first class work tolerated' is stamped on an unfinished piece, a collar, in Belfast Museum.

Unlike tamboured muslin, there was no work-room to be maintained, as the women worked in their own homes and were paid piece rates, not a

70. A worker's sampler, from Ayrshire, of needlemade lace stitches suitable for various spaces. Ayrshire embroidery (sewed muslin) is notable for the variety of fillings used on a single piece. (Miss S. Morris, Ayr)

weekly wage. Surprisingly, this fine work appears to have been done without a frame, not even a small hand frame. Unfinished pieces reveal that the

70a. Detail of fig. 70. The ordinary worker could earn a shilling a day if she worked steadily; those who specialized in lace stitches earned slightly more, hence the cost of a dress or cap depended on the number of lace insets.

solid embroidery, mostly satin stitch, was worked first. It was then handed to the lace workers, who received higher payment, and the spaces, already outlined with satin stitch, were cut away and needlepoint attached to the firm outline. A lacemaker's sampler survives (fig. 70), yellowed with age and use, divided into eighty inked squares, each filling numbered for reference. The fillings are arranged in groups according to the shape of the space they were designed to fill. One of the distinguishing marks of this Scottish whitework is the prodigal variety of fillings in the best pieces. Even tiny spaces in narrow borders reveal several different designs. On continental pieces, on the other hand, the same filling, in which the worker excelled, would generally be repeated, for the sake of speed.

In 1827, soon after she had started her new business, Mrs Jamieson applied to the Board of Trustees asking if she would be considered eligible for a premium. She was not so fortunate as Ruffini. The Trustees replied evasively, saying that though there was indeed a premium for embroidered muslin that year, yet they were doubtful whether 'even for that article you could be admitted a competitor, seeing that you are not the cloth manufacturer'. Undeterred, Mrs Jamieson replied by return, sending samples. She was told that they had been seen by some of the judges of the premium competition, and was invited to send an entry the following year. In addition, one of the Trustees had bought a collar in the parcel, for which he paid a guinea. The following year, Mrs Jamieson shared the first prize of £14 with Alexander Brown of Perth, a muslin manufacturer, for the best 'collars, tippets and pelerines'. A pelerine was the wide-shouldered fichu then fashionable.

In 1829 Mrs Jamieson sent collars, pelerines and baby dresses, which won a prize of £10. The baby dresses were voted 'equal to the French work of that description'. (Fig. 71.) Infants' gowns of sewed muslin have survived in large numbers, preserved out of sentiment and now used as christening gowns. The dresses, cut in the style of fashionable women's gowns of the late 1830s, with off-the-shoulder necklines, long skirt with inverted V-panel flanked by a flat frill or 'robing', and V-shaped bodice panel are characteristic of sewed muslin at its best. (Fig. 72.) They were eagerly bought by an increasingly prosperous middle class, who had maids to cope with the time-consuming ironing. Caps were worn by the infant by day and night. The night caps worn in the cradle were of plain cambric; the one worn by day could be delicately embroidered and trimmed with lace, with at the back a decorated crown to be displayed to admiration as the baby was carried around. (Figs 73 and 74.)

Mrs Jamieson was assisted in her business by her two daughters. One, Marian, married John Dalzell, who was also a cotton agent. When her

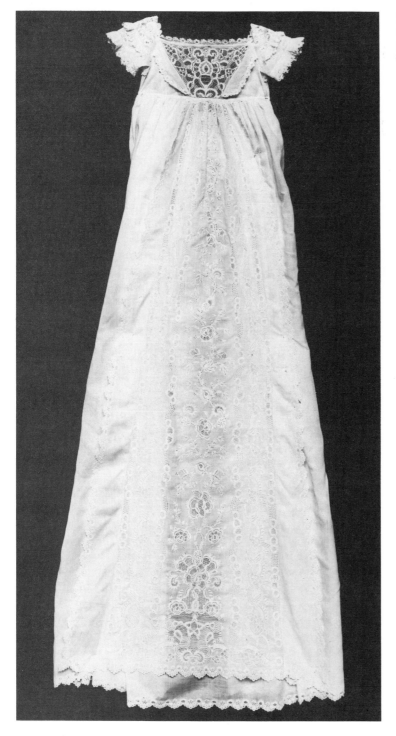

72. *Detail of the hem of a baby robe of Ayrshire embroidery, showing the variety of lace stitch fillings, and the decorated edging. The flat frill or 'robing' emphasizes the decorated central panel. (Mrs D. Arthur)*

first child was born the 'flo'orers' (those who flowered the muslin) made a robe said to be of the same design as one made and presented to Queen Victoria for the infant Prince of Wales, born 1841. It is now in the Royal Museum of Scotland.

As Ruffini had found, embroidery technique is easy to copy. Inevitably, Glasgow muslin manufacturers began to set up sewed muslin agencies for themselves. Possibly some of Mrs Jamieson's workers were persuaded to teach the technique to others. By 1837, out of 117 muslin manufacturers

in the Glasgow Directory, no less than 25 dealt in sewed muslin, chief of whom were John Mair & Co. and Alexander Wylie, as well as Brown, Sharp & Co. of Paisley. The professional designs and meticulous workmanship ensured that the Scottish sewed muslin could compete with French or continental whitework not only in Britain, but in Germany, Russia, and even in France itself. The craft spread to Ireland, where women were taught the skill. A firm in Donaghadee, Messrs Cochrane and Brown, distributed and collected the completed work. They eventually moved their offices to Glasgow, the export centre of the trade. A member of this firm was the first to employ the lithographic press, in 1837, to print the designs on to the muslin.

In his booklet *The Art of Ayrshire White*

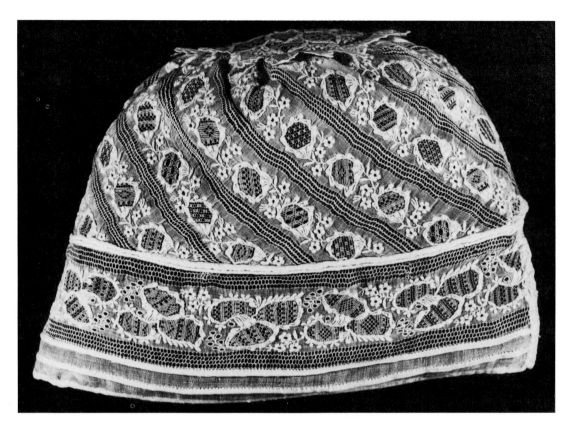

73. *Baby's cap of Ayrshire embroidery decorated with a variety of fillings. The caps were usually made of linen cambric rather than cotton muslin. The edge around the face would be decorated with lace frills and ribbons.* (Industrie und Gewerbemuseum, St Gallen, Switzerland)

Needlework, J.A. Morris condemned this move as contributing to the deterioration of the designs.[5] Certainly it must have proved useful in printing the miles of edging borders required. But Morris also denounced the practice that was standard in continental workrooms: that of different workers employed on different parts of the same piece – the lace workers, for instance, after the solid parts had been filled in. Apparently unaware of the true origin of the craft as set up by Mrs Jamieson, he drew a romantic and fictitious picture of Ayrshire women of the eighteenth century working fine embroidery of their own design on linen. Ignoring the fact that the baby robes are cut in the fashion of the late 1830s, he asserted that all the best work was done at this time (i.e. in the eighteenth century) before the work became 'commercialized'. From this, some museum curators have tended to rate the finer work as 'early', and work without much point lace as 'late'. In fact, the fineness or otherwise depended on the price paid.

Sewed muslin, or Ayrshire embroidery, as it came to be called, had acquired such importance that a paper on the subject was read to the British Association for the Advancement of Science, meeting at Belfast in 1857, possibly the only occasion when embroidery has appeared on the programme of that august society. J. Strang, in *The Embroidered Muslin Manufacture of Scotland and Ireland*, described in detail the organization and

74. Crown of the cap in fig. 73. This is a day cap, worn when the infant was carried around. The night cap worn in the cradle would be of plain cambric.

statistics of the industry, from the spinning of the yarn, the designing and printing of patterns, the distribution, collection and return of the work and the bleaching, to the making-up, boxing and marketing of the finished pieces.

1857 was also the last year of prosperity for sewed muslin, a prosperity that had lasted for thirty years. It was the year of a financial crisis in Glasgow, following on one in America, and several firms were forced to close. Four years later, with the outbreak of the American Civil War, supplies of raw cotton were almost cut off by the blockade imposed by the northern states, causing great hardship in Scotland and Lancashire. Muslin continued to be made and flowered in Scotland for another twenty years, but the industry withered from 1861. In Lancashire the cotton trade recovered after the end of the war, but the Scottish muslin manufacture depended on the ebb and flow of fashion. Fashion changed, but the final blow came from the machine-embroidered whitework imported from Switzerland, which gradually took over the market. The sewed muslin workers (or those that were left) transferred their skills to making collars and flounces on calico, without any lace stitch fillings. This coarser work, called broderie anglaise, sold for pitifully small sums. Even so, it still could not compete in price with white machine embroidery. The muslin trade was gradually forgotten in Scotland, though the exquisite whitework that embellished it survives to this day in the baby robes and caps still cherished in many families.

References

1. SRO, *The Minutes of the Board of Trustees for Fisheries and Manufactures for Scotland*, meeting on 18 June 1783.
2. C.G. de St Aubin., op.cit. p. 17. See Dr Johnson's *Dictionary*, 1755: *Tambour*: a frame resembling a drum, on which a kind of embroidery is worked; the embroidery so made.' See also: M. Swain, 'Tamboured muslin in Scotland', *Embroidery* Vol. XIV no. 1., Spring 1963, p. 20.
3. The Trustees' Academy eventually became the Edinburgh College of Art.
4. *Caledonian Mercury*, 28 September 1782.
5. J.A. Morris, *The Art of Ayrshire White Needlework*, Glasgow, 1916, written to celebrate an exhibition of needlework in aid of the Red Cross. The author is also responsible for the legend that the workers bathed their eyes in whisky.

CHAPTER EIGHT

Scottish Samplers

Plain sewing – hemming, running, seaming and whipping – were skills needed by every housewife, though there were some so poor that they had no chance to learn these essential accomplishments unless they became maidservants, where they could be taught by mistress or housekeeper. Until the middle of the eighteenth century, linen was generally bought by the ell (a Scottish ell was 37 inches, 94 cm) and made up at home into sheets, tablecloths, napkins, shirts and shifts. Everyone who could sew helped with the task. In 1598 the Wardrobe at Balloch (now Taymouth Castle) contained, among the linen in use, 98 serviettes 'maid by the Ladie of new lynnings, and 3 doz. markit with blew silk'.[1]

A century later, at Mellerstain, Lady Grisell Baillie set her maids to spin lint (flax fibre) that was woven into sheeting by a weaver, and then sent to a bleachfield for bleaching. She also bought woven linen by the ell for sheets. Linen damask for tablecloths and 'servits' (table napkins) was purchased at Inverkeithing Fair in Fife and at other centres. Muslin and calico was bought and made into underwear and nightclothes. In 1695 she paid £48 Scots for holland for her husband's shirts. It was only in 1740 that she records buying shirts 'rady made' for her grandson George, Lord Binning, when he went to Oxford as an undergraduate.

Not everyone possessed the stores of linen that were needed in large houses such as Balloch and Mellerstain, where tablecloths and napkins were marked in sets, and sheets numbered to use in rotation. But anyone who aspired to becoming mistress, or at least maid, in a prosperous house-

hold needed to learn how to mark sheets and tablecloths with fine cross stitch. Moreover, while making a cross stitch alphabet upon a sampler, a little girl was also learning her letters and numbers. A sampler at Blair Castle shows how 'Catherine Walker ag^d 6', learned her multiplication tables in addition to neat cross stitch. (Fig. 75.)

Samplers were used for other purposes than learning 'marking stitch'. Not all of them were made by children. Some record patterns, collected by an adult in the same way as cookery recipes. The so-called 'spot' samplers of the seventeenth century show these trial motifs, often unfinished, recording a complicated stitch or unit of a pattern that could be combined into a continuous repeating design. These samplers, usually undated and unmarked, are generally described as English. Similar stitch records must have been made in Scotland also, although no spot sampler with a firm Scottish provenance has been located.

There are, of course, many samplers made by adults in Scotland as well as in England, bearing patterns worked in the soft Berlin wools popular in the nineteenth century. These are often on long narrow strips, trial pieces to work out a colour combination or stitch. By no means all of them are in cross stitch, nor are all the designs Victorian. They often include repeating patterns of a century earlier, perhaps copied from an old chair cover.

Trade samplers, which also belong to this group of adult samplers, occasionally survive, but they are much rarer, since they were generally destroyed with the books when the firm closed down. A length of white cotton muslin, now in the Royal Museum of Scotland, shows some thirty designs,

MULTIPLICATION TABLE

1	2	3	4	5	6	7	8	9	10	11	12
2	4	6	8	10	12	14	16	18	20	22	24
3	6	9	12	15	18	21	24	27	30	33	36
4	8	12	16	20	24	28	32	36	40	44	48
5	10	15	20	25	30	35	40	45	50	55	60
6	12	18	24	30	36	42	48	54	60	66	72
7	14	21	28	35	42	49	56	63	70	77	84
8	16	24	32	40	48	56	64	72	80	88	96
9	18	27	36	45	54	63	72	81	90	99	108
10	20	30	40	50	60	70	80	90	100	110	120
11	22	33	44	55	66	77	88	99	110	121	132
12	24	36	48	60	72	84	96	108	120	132	144

CATHARINE WALKER AG^d 6

75. Sampler in the form of a multiplication table, signed 'Catherine Walker ag^d 6'. Cross stitch and double running stitch on linen. Undated, probably about 1800. (The Duke of Atholl)

worked in chain stitch with a tambour hook and numbered in Turkey red cotton, that could be ordered from a firm in Old Cumnock, Ayrshire around 1810. They include kerchief corners and designs for the hems of ladies' dresses. (See fig. 68.)

Most of the samplers that survive, however, are the work of children. They have been preserved for sentimental reasons, often in the family of the little girl who made them. They are attractive to collectors and to antique dealers, since they are small, are framed so that they may be displayed on a wall, are often dated, and have a naïve charm. Scottish samplers of the eighteenth and nineteenth centuries abound: indeed, the making of a sampler appears to have been an essential part of a Scottish girl's schooling until about 1900. Boys' samplers also survive. Usually the first sampler was a simple

76. *The Mellerstain Panel. Signed and dated* 'GB RB MM 1706'. *The initials are those of Grisell Baillie, born 1692, Rachel Baillie her sister, born 1696, and May Menzies, their governess. All the motifs are taken from* A Booke of Beast, Flowers, Fruits, Flies and Wormes, *published by Thomas Johnson, London 1630. The centrepiece shows 'Smelling' copied from* engravings of the 'Five Senses' bound into the volume. The flowers and animals have all been chosen from different pages of the book. Coloured wools and silks on a blue ground worked in fine tent stitch on canvas. 33×49.5 cm/$13 \times 19\frac{1}{2}$ in. (The Earl of Haddington, KT)

affair of alphabets and numbers, with one or two motifs. The second sampler was much more accomplished, and it is this that has generally been cherished, first by its maker (who sometimes unpicked the tell-tale age and date), and then by her descendants.

The pictorial panel at Mellerstain made in 1706 by Grisell and Rachel, the two daughters of Lady Grisell Baillie, under the direction of their governess, May Menzies, has always been called a sampler by the family, although it is a tent stitch picture of the type so popular in the seventeenth century. (Fig. 76.) It is a key piece in establishing the use of the engraved sources of the designs that occur so frequently on these pictures. By a happy chance, the book of engravings from which all the motifs have been traced, and which belonged to May Menzies, has been preserved at Mellerstain along with the panel. The book (fig. 77), published in London in 1630, had been brought back to

IIO

Labels on image: *Cyanus* Blew Bottle. | *Mala strantia.* | Oranges | Mountaine Lillies. | *Martagon.* | *Falco.*

Scotland by May Menzies's grandfather, the Revd William Colt, the outspoken Presbyterian minister of Inveresk near Edinburgh, as a present for his wife, Katherine Logan, whose initials *KL* are stamped on the vellum binding. (Fig. 78.)

When Grisell and Rachel worked this finely executed panel, they were aged fourteen and ten, and the panel was no doubt the triumphant

78. Page from A Booke of Beast . . . *The rhinoceros and the falcon have been copied from this page on to the panel. (*The Earl of Haddington, KT*)*

successor to earlier, less assured samplers by the two girls. The next year, they began other embroideries, as Lady Grisell's accounts reveal:

Edinburgh 1707
May. To $\frac{1}{4}$ whit satin for the bairenses satin
pece   £1. 2. 6
 For silks to it, 6s. nails, threed to the tent
[frame]   7. 0
 For silk to make a purs and strings   13. 0

The satin piece used up more silk than expected, for in August there was another entry:

77. Engraving: 'Smelling', from the 'Five Senses'. A countrywoman with a basket and nosegay of sweet-smelling flowers is accompanied by a dog, the animal symbol of the sense of smell, on account of his keen scent. (The Earl of Haddington, KT)

Aug. 26. For silk to the children's satine piece (Mrs. Miller)   £3. 12. 0

This was probably an ambitious piece of raised work on white satin, to be worked on a frame, or tent. The 'satin piece' has unfortunately not survived. The flowers and beasts pictured in May Menzies' book would have furnished suitable designs for this embroidery as well.

The samplers of a young Glasgow girl illustrate the way a middle-class daughter perfected her needlework. She was born in 1806. Her father was Andrew Gardner, a mathematical optician of Candleriggs, Glasgow. It is not known where Elizabeth went to school. Her first sampler of 1818 bears three alphabets in red and green silk, the last in ornate capitals worked in eyelet stitch, and displaying a curiously archaic letter A. Below the coronet of king, duke, marquis and baron are the initials of her parents and family. (Fig. 79.)

Elizabeth's second sampler, worked when she was fourteen years old, is much more assured. There are three alphabets, one in lower case. Another is very ornate, the letters embellished with double running stitch (Holbein stitch). This curiously old-fashioned stitch is used on two rows of designs, dating from the seventeenth century and copied from earlier samplers. A tree, together with strawberries, is flanked by a pair of peacocks with six tail feathers, and her parents' initials, *A G* and *E J*. (Fig. 80.)

Elizabeth's sampler of 1821 is much more unusual. (Fig. 81.) Worked in blocks of red and green silk, there are trial pieces in the stitches employed in drawn muslin embroidery: so-called Dresden work, generally worked in white on fine white satin muslin (see fig. 66), but here worked without tension on a loose linen scrim. This technique can be seen on white samplers, especially in Scandinavia, but the idea of teaching the stitches on a coarser scrim, in colour, appears to have been usual in Scotland, as several samplers of this type are known, as well as one, presumably Irish, dated 1793 in the Ulster Museum, Belfast.

The final sampler made by Elizabeth Gardner is

81. Sampler, signed and dated 'Elizabeth Gardner Glasgow 1821'. Drawn fabric ('pulled') stitch fillings, suitable for Dresden work. Red and green silks on linen. 22.5 × 15.2 cm/8¾ × 6 in. (Miss S.G. Muirhead)

pattern for the crown of a baby's cap, still to be found, at that late date, decorated with this fine and intricate stitch. In another twenty years Ayrshire embroidery, with its elaborate and varied fillings, would have superseded the ancient hollie point. Each block on this sampler is neatly outlined with dark blue satin ribbon, a method of mounting found on other samplers of this type. In other Scottish families successive samplers by the same girl have been preserved, but Elizabeth's series of four must be regarded as a record. Only the four pieces by an English girl, Martha Edlin, born in 1660, are comparable. These are now in the Victoria & Albert Museum, and consist of a sampler of alphabets in coloured silks, a white cutwork sampler dated 1669, a raised work casket of 1671 and a jewel case of beadwork, rococo and tent stitches dated 1673.

It is often asked how a Scottish sampler may be distinguished. Apart from the obvious clues of a Scottish surname, such as McNab, or a Scottish location, like the 'Glasgow' on Elizabeth Gardner's first and second samplers, there are certain other characteristics by which a Scottish sampler may be recognized. Marcus Huish, in his book *Samplers and Tapestry Embroideries* (1900), suggests that 'bright colouring, coarsish canvas, and ornate lettering . . . suggest a Scottish origin'.[2] There is, however, more reliable evidence to be found. On many of them, the initials or the whole names of the child's parents appear. Thus, on her first sampler of 1818, Elizabeth Gardner worked *A G* and *E G* for her parents Andrew and Elizabeth Gardner, followed by the initials of her half-sister and two brothers.

In Scotland, however, unlike England, a woman retains her maiden name after she marries. It is written into all legal documents, with her husband's surname as an alternative. Indeed, it is frequently carved on her gravestone. Although her mother's surname has not been discovered, Elizabeth appears to be following the Scottish practice in her second sampler, where her parents' initials appear as *A G* and *E J*.

There is no ambiguity, however, in the ambi-

white on white: a small square of four damask darning patterns, and four blocks of needlemade lace fillings. The centrepiece contains a medallion of hollie point with a crown, the initials *E G* and the date 1822. (Fig. 82.) Indeed, it offers a useful

82. *Sampler, signed and dated 'EG 1822'. Darning patterns and needlepoint lace fillings with crown, date and initials in the centre medallion worked in hollie point. Framed and divided by dark blue satin ribbon. 15.2 × 13.9 cm/6 × 5½ in. (Miss S.G. Muirhead)*

tious sampler inscribed 'Catherine McDonal sewed this semplar with Janet Anderson 1822'.[3] The full names of Catherine's parents, John McDonald and Mary McCallum, surmounted by crowns, occupy compartments left and right.

Below is Duncan McCallum Senner (Senior), probably her maternal grandfather. Beside the moral verse are other family initials. (Fig. 83.) Such samplers are priceless genealogical records of the family that still owns one. It is possible to see how many of the family were alive at the time the sampler was made. The initials of those who have died are frequently worked in black. Much thought must have gone into the choice of these initials, for aunts and uncles, even family friends were often included. One little girl, whose mother had died, worked her mother's initials in black, her

83. Sampler inscribed 'Catherine McDonal sewed this semplar with Janet Anderson 1822', with the names of Catherine's parents, John McDonald and Mary McCallum, and Duncan McCallum Senner (Senior), probably her maternal grandfather. Other family initials are included with, below, a building labelled 'Inverary Castle', probably copied from an engraving. 55 × 52 cm/21¾ × 20½ in. (Trustees of the Royal Museum of Scotland)

stepmother's in colour, and her father, who was still alive, but technically a widower, was also inscribed in black.[4] Another child, who was illegitimate, substituted the initials of her grand-parents, who had given her a loving home, in the place of her mother.

This custom of using the mother's maiden surname is often the means of establishing the

116

84. *Engraving:* Inverary Castle. *Plate XVI from* A Tour in Scotland, *1759, (Pennant). Third edition 1774, printed by W. Ayres, Warrington. (*Royal Commission on the Ancient and Historical Monuments of Scotland*)

provenance of a Scottish sampler. The parents of Margret Boog, who sewed her sampler in 1761, both had unusual names: Robert Boog and Margret Orrock. (Colour plate VIII.) It has been possible to discover that they married in the Canongate Church, Edinburgh in 1743. Margret Orrock's father was a cutler who, in 1739, sharpened the blade of the Duke of Gordon's sword, and supplied him with a new scabbard for it.[5] Robert Boog was also a cutler, who became Deacon of the Guild of Hammermen, the guild of metalworkers in Edinburgh. He and his son set up a flourishing business which continued into the nineteenth century, supplying ivory-handled knives to the Scottish gentry and instruments such as scalpels to the surgeons of Edinburgh. It has not

85. Sampler signed and dated 'Mary Butler Stark Kingsdale 1803', with the inscription 'Favour is deceitful and beauty is vain but a woman that feareth the Lord shall be praise'. This was Mary's second sampler, made when she was nine years old. Kinsale House, shown on the sampler, was sold in 1803 and rebuilt, so this is the only view of the house as it was. Cross stitch in coloured wools on woollen canvas. 35.5 × 34.5/14 × 13½ in. (Mrs John Kerr)

been possible, however, to find out where Margret Boog went to school. There were several private schools for young ladies in Edinburgh at that time. In 1768 Margret married a tailor, James Murray, and went to live in Haddington, near Edinburgh.

The buildings that occur on Scottish samplers are often thought to be imaginary. The five-storeyed house on Margret Boog's sampler, complete with man wearing a tricorne hat and carrying a staff, appears on several samplers dating from 1761 to the 1830s, but has not so far been identified on any print or engraving. Catherine McDonald's stately edifice permits no ambiguity, for she has labelled it 'Inverary Castle'. Although dwarfed by the birds on either side, it is a good representation, within the limits of cross stitch, of the central block of the castle, designed for the third Duke of Argyll by Roger Morris, though the wall and flanking lodges never existed. It seems likely that Catherine took the design from a print, for her family is not to be found in the parish register of Inverary. (See fig. 84.)

Another little girl, Mary Butler Stark, worked her first sampler in 1801. It records the names of her parents, James Stark and Mary Butler, as well as other members of her family. Her second sampler, made in 1803 when she was nine years old, shows her home, Kingsdale in Fife. (Fig. 85.) That same year it was sold and rebuilt, so that Mary's sampler is now the only record of the house as once it was. Other samplers show houses now demolished. It seems probable that the solid symmetrical houses appearing on many Scottish samplers between 1750 and 1850 are not imaginary but actual houses, too familiar to the needlewoman and her family to need a label.

Mary's first sampler is worked on linen scrim; her second has suffered some moth damage and is worked on a woollen canvas known as tammy (tamis), or boulting cloth. This was easily available, as it was used for straining sauces and for sifting flour, not only in mills, but in the domestic kitchen. In 1745 a woman was hired at Gordon Castle, Aberdeenshire, to help sieve the bran from the flour:

James Ker's relict [widow] Margaret McBane wrought nine days in the Scalry [scullery] while Jean Jamison Scalry woman was employed Boulting Flower and other works as is attested by me at the rate of two pence pr. day. Archibald Anderson.[6]

Only one motif appearing on Scottish samplers may be described as exclusively Scottish. This is a crowned thistle, enclosed in an octagonal medallion surrounded by the words 'I have power to defend myself and others' (fig. 86), a more aggressive version of the motto 'Nemo me impune lacessit'. Many other favourite motifs are common to the rest of Britain. The border with twisted stems at the top of Catherine Macdonald's sampler may be seen at the top of Margret Boog's and Janet Learmonth's. It appears on a sampler dated 1762 in plate XXIII of Marcus Huish's book, which he ascribes to Robert Henderson, because 'that is not only the first [name] but is worked in a darker silk'. In fact, Robert Henderson and Jean Henderson were probably the parents of Cristan Henderson, whose name appears below. It seems likely that Robert Henderson, worked in black silk, was dead when the sampler was worked.

This border with twisted stems remained popular in Scotland till the 1850s. It can be seen on many English samplers and even appears on one of the earliest American examples – that of Lora, daughter of Miles Standish, worked before 1655, and now belonging to the Pilgrim Society, Massachussetts. Lora Standish's sampler also shows the stiff row of pinks or carnations that is worked above the names of Robert Boog and Margret Orrock. Instead of growing out of a two-handled vase, Lora's pinks are supported by an interlaced knot, a variation found on others spread over two centuries.

A peacock with seven (occasionally eight or six) tail feathers is regarded as peculiarly Scottish. Though this bird is rare on English samplers, it is found on many Scandinavian examples. A colour scheme of red and green was popular, particularly for the first alphabet sampler, but no doubt this depended on the colours available.

86. Sampler inscribed 'Janet Learmonth at Mrs. Nimmos', in pale fawn silk above the lower border. On the left is the Black Dog part of the Linlithgow arms with the motto 'Fear God and Honour the King'. Right is a crowned thistle in an octagon with the motto 'I have power to defend myself and others' and the date 1765. Compare the top border and the building with Margaret Boog's sampler. (Miss S.G. Muirhead)

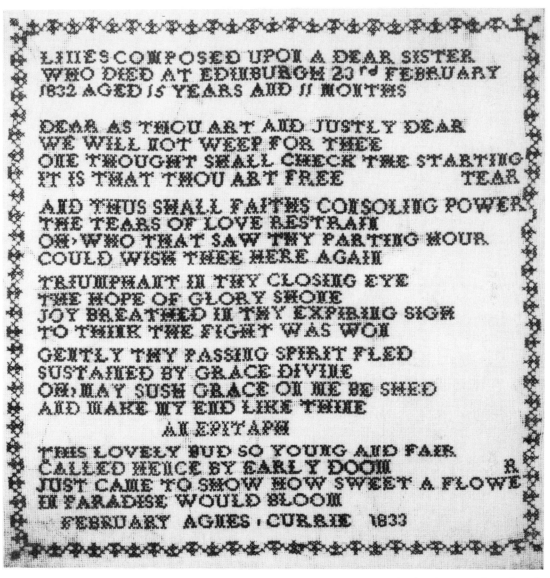

LINES COMPOSED UPON A DEAR SISTER
WHO DIED AT EDINBURGH 23rd FEBRUARY
1832 AGED 15 YEARS AND 11 MONTHS

DEAR AS THOU ART AND JUSTLY DEAR
WE WILL NOT WEEP FOR THEE
ONE THOUGHT SHALL CHECK THE STARTING
IT IS THAT THOU ART FREE   TEAR

AND THUS SHALL FAITHS CONSOLING POWER
THE TEARS OF LOVE RESTRAIN
OH, WHO THAT SAW THY PARTING HOUR
COULD WISH THEE HERE AGAIN

TRIUMPHANT IN THY CLOSING EYE
THE HOPE OF GLORY SHONE
JOY BREATHED IN THY EXPIRING SIGH
TO THINK THE FIGHT WAS WON

GENTLY THY PASSING SPIRIT FLED
SUSTAINED BY GRACE DIVINE
OH, MAY SUCH GRACE ON ME BE SHED
AND MAKE MY END LIKE THINE

                AN EPITAPH

THIS LOVELY BUD SO YOUNG AND FAIR
CALLED HENCE BY EARLY DOOM
JUST CAME TO SHOW HOW SWEET A FLOWE R
IN PARADISE WOULD BLOOM
        FEBRUARY AGNES · CURRIE 1833

87. *Memorial sampler, signed and dated 'February Agnes Currie 1833', and inscribed 'Lines composed upon a dear sister who died at Edinburgh 23rd February 1832 aged 15 years and 11 months'. Black silk cross stitch on canvas. 14 cm/5½ in. square. (Miss Fiona Dunnett)*

Since children in Scotland were accustomed to learning the metrical Psalms by heart, it might be expected that these would appear on Scottish samplers, but curiously they have not been found. Instead, the verses and texts are similar to those chosen elsewhere in the English-speaking world, with the verse:

Jesus permit Thy gracious name to stand
As the first effort of an infant's hand . . .

a favourite. Equally popular was the rhymed version of the Ten Commandments from Dr Isaac

Watts' *Divine Songs for Children* (1715):

Have thou no other Gods but Me,
Unto no image bend thy knee . . .

A verse found on some Edinburgh samplers is less devout than most. In 1791 Elizabeth Cotton promised:

All you my friends who now expect to see
A piece of marking thus Perform'd by me
Cast but a Smile on this my mean Endeavour,
I'll Strive to Mend and be Obedient ever.

Samplers continued to be made in Scottish schools up to 1900, richly embellished with family initials. Some were rolled up and forgotten; others were framed and displayed with pride. One mother viewed her daughter's work without sentiment. When twelve-year-old Sarah Wilson proudly took home from Sandford School near Strathaven her neatly worked sampler in 1878, her mother roundly declared that she would 'frame nae clout' and told her to take it back to school to fill in the background. This Sarah obediently did, filling in the background with a light brown cross stitch. Only then did her mother consider the sampler worthy of framing. Sarah lived till 1948 and told the story to her descendants, who cherish the sampler.

Occasionally a sampler was made, not as evidence of skill, but to commemorate a loved one. One made in Edinburgh is only $5\frac{1}{2}$ inches square. It is worked in cross stitch in black silk and is inscribed:

Lines composed upon a dear sister who died at Edinburgh 23 February 1832. Aged 15 years and 11 months.

There are four verses, ending:

This lovely bud so young and fair
Called hence by early doom
Just came to show how sweet a flower
In Paradise would bloom.
February Agnes Currie 1833 (Fig. 87.)

This disciplined austere needlework is the Scottish equivalent of the memorial picture, with mourning figures around a sepulchre beneath weeping willows, in which American needlewomen expressed their grief.

Little girls in Scotland, therefore, like their counterparts in the rest of Britain and America, painstakingly copied patterns from old samplers furnished by their teachers, but in Scotland there was a strong tradition of family sentiment, so that the initials of parents, brothers, sisters and even friends and grandparents, transformed the sampler into a touching family document.

References
1. C. Innes, (ed.), *The Black Book of Taymouth*, Bannatyne Club, 1855, p. 327.
2. M. Huish, *Samplers and Tapestry Embroideries*, 1900, plate XVIII.
3. N. Tarrant, *Samplers*, The Royal Scottish Museum, 1978, plate 43.
4. I am indebted to Mrs J.M. Fulton, Breckish, Isle of Skye, for this information.
5. SRO Gordon Papers GD44/51/465/1/66. Note that the widow of James Ker is given her maiden name.
6. Ibid. GD/44/51/260/1/11.

CHAPTER NINE

Victorian Embroidery

Although Queen Victoria did not succeed to the throne of Great Britain and Ireland until 1837, it has been customary to dismiss the entire nineteenth century as 'Victorian', and its embroidery as trite and tasteless.[1] As we approach the end of the twentieth century, this attitude demands reappraisal. The wide popularity of the printed patterns for Berlin wool work in cross stitch on canvas is blamed for the supposed decline in design and technique. As we have seen, the domestic needlewoman of the past did not consider it necessary to invent her own designs, but relied heavily on patterns drawn out for her by the professional. She could trace a design from a printed book, as on the Mellerstain panel, or use a design drawn by a gifted amateur, like Henrietta Cumming. No matter how skilled her sewing techniques, or how wide her repertoire of stitches, the domestic needlewoman was aware of her limitations and preferred a professionally drawn design to one of her own contriving. However ardently she desired to be fashionable, she felt no necessity to be 'original'.

There were many reasons for the popularity of Berlin wool work. First, the printed patterns became available to the most isolated needlewoman, especially after the new improved postal service was instituted in 1840. With wools for working, they could even be sent overseas. The Marchioness of Dalhousie (1817–53), whose husband was Governor General of India from 1848 to 1856, had panels and wools sent to her by her mother and sisters. She was an enthusiastic needlewoman, and her work included flower pieces and biblical subjects: the traditional

favourites such as *The Finding of Moses* and *Jephtha's Daughter*, as well as the up-to-date *Scottish Gamekeeper* and *English Gamekeeper* by Landseer. She accompanied her husband on all his official journeys, even to parts of the Himalayas where no European woman had ever before visited. Although an excellent horsewoman, rapidly failing health eventually compelled her to travel in a litter. A sketch survives, showing her with her hat shading her eyes, stitching busily, borne on a litter by four servants.

Her mother, the Marchioness of Tweeddale, and her sisters, were also skilled needlewomen. They began a large carpet worked in squares, intended for the drawing room of Dalhousie Castle, to be made for her return. A hearth rug and several squares of the carpet have survived, with a design of roses and passion flowers, worked on a delicate green ground. Sadly, the health of Lady Dalhousie declined so rapidly that she was sent home from India in the hope that the sea voyage would revive her, but she died before reaching England. The carpet was put away unfinished. (Fig. 88.)

The printed designs were not, as is sometimes implied, easy options for the lazy needlewoman. A design inked on to canvas, especially when outlined with black silk, as it was for Mary, Queen of Scots, or on the Traquair 'slips', did not make undue demands on the skill of the worker, though it left scope for the choosing of her own colours. It was, indeed, the method still preferred in France, as the Countess of Wilton pointed out in her book, *The Art of Needlework* (1840). The Berlin pattern with its tiny coloured squares required unremitting

88. *Panel, Berlin wool work on canvas. The ground is worked in two shades of pale green. One of five squares intended for a carpet for the drawing room at Dalhousie Castle. It was worked by the mother and sisters of the Marchioness of Dalhousie, but was put away unfinished after her untimely death in 1853. 89 cm/35 in. square. (Lady Broun Lindsay)*

89. *Panel for a screen:* The Scottish Gamekeeper, *after Landseer. Wool cross stitch on canvas. This and its companion piece,* The English Gamekeeper, *were popular Berlin wool work patterns. One of twelve panels worked by twelve young ladies in the Carse of Gowrie, they were incorporated into a wooden screen that was raffled in order to raise funds to establish a school for the daughters of ministers of the Church of Scotland.*

concentration, for a miscount could throw the whole design out, and the complicated shading must have been exacting to work by the light of a lamp. A far greater realism could be obtained by using the charts, however. The flowers were more life-like: the plumage of birds could be rendered with fidelity. To the Victorian, this was important. A later age, with other tastes, dismisses them as 'representational'. (Fig. 89.)

Squared designs for needlework were by no means novel. They had appeared in the earliest printed pattern books. The chief charm of this Victorian needlework lay in the so-called Berlin wools from which it took its name. The soft wools, with long silky staple, which absorbed dye readily, came from Saxony, where the Elector had improved the flocks by the introduction in 1765 of merino sheep from Spain. The wools were dyed in Berlin in a wide range of brilliant colours that could be highlighted with silk or beads. They were delightful to use, filling the canvas smoothly, though for chairs and stools many needlewomen continued to employ the harder-wearing worsteds. The dyes used were not at the outset aniline, for Perkin's 'mauvine', the first aniline dye, was not introduced till 1856, to be followed by 'magenta' in 1860. Those who condemn them for their vividness, extolling the subtle shades of the old vegetable dyestuffs, forget that the colours we see on earlier embroideries, particularly chair covers and the like, are exceedingly faded. The backs of such covers, or the unused 'slips' at Traquair, ought to remind us how bright, even strident, some of the old dyes were when the threads were first used.

For all their popularity, Berlin patterns did not oust other forms of needlework in Scotland. It was still possible, in Edinburgh as in other cities, to get designs drawn out to order, and professional embroiderers still undertook commissions decorating military uniforms, colours and the like. Even the professional, however, used Berlin wools on occasion. In 1842 the firm of A. Müller, 43 and 44 Princes Street, Edinburgh, Manufacturers and Importers from Berlin, had supplied a needlework screen of eight panels to the Duchess of Buccleuch.

The Duchess refused to pay their bill, saying that she understood the price to have been £5 per panel, totalling £40 in all, and placed the matter in the hands of the family solicitor in Edinburgh. After investigation, he wrote to the Duke that Müllers claimed that no price had been mentioned when the screen was commissioned, and that their bill was based on the charge of one shilling for each thousand stitches, adding, 'I understand the stitches are easily counted by taking one row each way and multiplying the sums into each other.' A month later, the bill still in dispute, Müllers 'expressed a willingness that the work should be referred to any person accustomed to deal in such articles and to abide by her decision'. The solicitor proposed Madame Gauguin as the referee, and that one of the panels should be sent in from Bowhill for her inspection. It is not known how the matter was finally settled.

It is significant of the change that had taken place over the previous century that the leading professional embroiderer should be no longer male, but female. The decline of the professional workshops in the eighteenth century had coincided with an increase in schools for young ladies, to judge by the newspaper advertisements that emphasized the teaching of embroidery. To cater for the needs of these amateur needlewomen, specialist shops, offering lessons as well as materials, had opened, similar to one advertised in Edinburgh in 1797:

ARCHDEACON, Miss. No.1 East Register Street
Teaches the following arts, viz, drawing, embroidery & all sorts of fancy work. M.A. draws patterns colours and shades them ready to work, so as any lady deficient in painting may complete the piece herself.
N.B. All sorts of materials such as embroidery, silks, shanails, ribbons, worsted in shades, etc. may be had at her house. M.A. informs the public that the above work and articles are superior to any that can be had from London.

Madame Jane Gauguin, who had been appointed arbitrator between the Duchess of Buccleuch and the firm of Müller, seems to have been the widow of John James Gauguin, who in 1823 had a warehouse for French blond lace, artificial flowers, etc. at 63 North Bridge Street. He was also a maker of braids. The firm moved to the more fashionable George Street in 1825, and remained there dealing in fancy work till 1860, when it became an embroidery warehouse under Miss Isabella Crooks. Madame Gauguin was well known for her books of instruction on *Knitting, Netting and Crochet Work (The Lady's Assistant)*, with an appendix on canvas work. The second series, published in 1842, prints an impressive list of 'Patronesses and Subscribers', beginning with Her Majesty the Queen Dowager (Queen Adelaide), three Royal Highnesses and seven Duchesses, including the Duchess of Buccleuch, and continuing through six pages of lesser ladies. In her Preface, the author trusts 'that it will not only be found a book of fashionable amusement to the higher ranks of society, but also a repertory of useful Receipts to the more humble'. The sixth edition (1844) was published by Ackermann & Co., Strand, London, as well as by the author in Edinburgh.

Other professional embroiderers, mostly female, are listed in the Edinburgh Directories. They undertook needlework of all descriptions but especially white embroidery, such as the making of handkerchiefs and household linen to order. A sample book of edges and monograms drawn out by Agnes Quintin Dalrymple for the business run by her mother and aunts between 1834 and 1876 shows initials suitable for handkerchiefs marked '6 Pence', while smaller plainer initials are only '3 Pence'. The firm, E. & C. McConnell, George Street, appears as 'Embroiderers, Dressmakers and Milliners' from 1834. From 1867 to 1876 it is described as 'Embroiderer, Lace Maker and Transferer'.

A firm that survived for over a century in Edinburgh, only closing in 1939, was that of Mrs and Miss Bowie. They specialized in white embroidery, undertaking the decoration and initialling of clothing and household linens. Their trade sampler (fig. 90) shows the quality of their work. They also dealt in sewed muslin, selling not only complete garments, but items such as cap crowns, bodices and edging, so that baby clothes could be made up at home.

Throughout the century, printed designs were readily available, first in such publications as the *Lady's Magazine*, which first began publishing embroidery designs in 1770. These publications increased in number as the century advanced. There was, for instance, the well-known journal, the *Englishwoman's Domestic Magazine*, published by Samuel Beaton, which included folded plates of coloured needlework patterns between 1861 and 1864. Embroidery worked in Scotland had become indistinguishable from that of the rest of Britain.

Modest homes in Scotland, as well as great mansions, were decorated with needlework. An unrecorded and often hidden embroidery is to be found on old Scots blankets. These were heavy, double length, and of a twill weave, usually with one or two blue stripes woven below the hem. They were embellished with simple flower shapes, but more often, large circles were worked in surface stitches in coloured wool along the hem. It is not clear whether these decorated blankets were used instead of bedcovers, or whether the decoration was intended to be revealed when the bedcover was removed. Since the blankets were not intended for show, most have worn out or been cut up. They should not, however, be regarded merely as Victorian 'fancy work', for a twill-woven blanket embroidered in coloured woollen threads bears in the centre the initials *IC* for Isabella Carmicael, and the date 1705.[2] (Fig. 91.)

Blankets decorated with large circles survive in America, where they are called 'rose blankets'. The heavy twill of Scots blankets makes a more suitable ground for stitchery than the fluffier lighter fabric of English blankets, though the term 'rose' or 'rosed' was also applied to the mark or stop woven at intervals along a stockful of twenty English blankets to indicate the position for cutting or

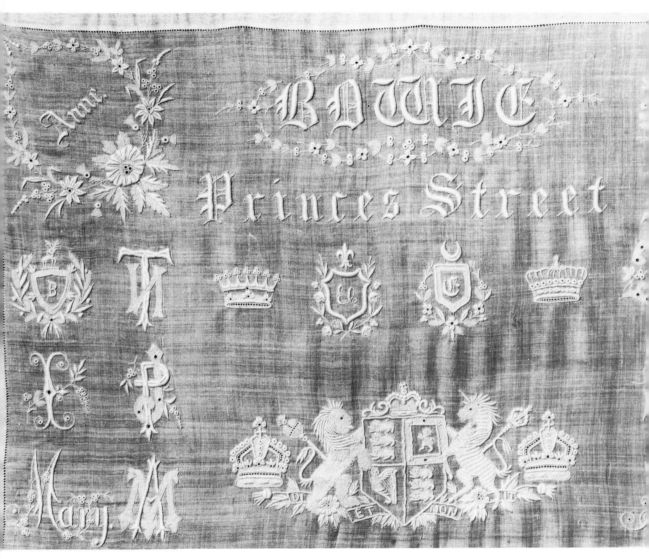

90. *Trade sampler of the firm of Mrs and Miss Bowie, muslin printers and embroiderers of Princes Street, Edinburgh, from 1839 to 1939. About 1860. (The Trustees of the Royal Museum of Scotland)*
91. *Embroidered blanket, consisting of two widths of twill-weave Scots blanket, joined down the centre,* and embroidered in coloured wools with the date 1705 and initials IC, for Isabel Carmichael. Embroidered Scots blankets continued to be made in the nineteenth century, but the decoration is confined to the hem and sides in surviving examples. 170 × 213 cm/67 × 84 in. (The Trustees of the Royal Museum of Scotland)

tearing the length into individual blankets of about ninety inches long.[3]

An embroidered blanket may have been re-

garded as an alternative to the patchwork quilt which, surprisingly, is seldom found in Scotland, perhaps because of the difficulty of accommodat-

128

ing a large frame for the quilting that, properly speaking, should hold the patchwork top and the lining together. Cotton and silk patchwork was certainly made, but is generally utilitarian, and does not compare with the lively and decorative designs achieved in North America.

A curious and exacting type of patchwork was executed by men. Although not exclusive to Scotland, it is well documented here. It is made of firm, well-fulled woollen materials, broadcloth, tweed and frieze, often tailors' clippings: indeed those who made it were frequently tailors, though soldiers and sailors, using snippets of uniform materials, also made these heavy panels. The earliest known of these panels – it seems improbable that they were intended as bedcovers, because of the weight – is at Sissinghurst Castle, Kent, dated 1761, and bears the Royal Arms with profiles of King George III and Queen Charlotte.

The Scottish panels belong to the middle of the nineteenth century. The designs derive from popular theatrical prints, the 'penny plain, twopence coloured' variety, that were published by such firms as Pollock, Reddington and Skelt in London, who also sold toy theatres with card scenery and actors. Series of famous generals and royalty were also available. A popular pastime was 'tinselling' these prints. Coloured tinsel shapes, cut as crowns, breastplates, stars, etc. could be bought to decorate them. The figures on the patchwork follow the printed model so closely that it may be assumed that the original print was cut up, with the outline of each part used as a template for the chosen material.

This 'tailors' patchwork' is executed with superlative skill. The thick cloth is not applied to a fabric foundation, as are the Newliston panels, nor is it turned in, as in ordinary 'pieced' patchwork. Instead, the shapes are meticulously cut and joined edge-to-edge with invisible stitches. It is, indeed, a fabric version of the art of marquetry in wood, except that, unlike wood, the cloth is not stuck down to any foundation, and the edges would fray unless they were neatly and firmly sewn to the surrounding material.

It is a technique scarcely attempted by the amateur needlewoman, but it was used in professional workshops for large pieces such as altar frontals and bedhangings in the sixteenth and seventeenth centuries.[4] It seems unlikely, however, that the men who made these panels were aware of its earlier use, but panels found in Wales and elsewhere show that the skill was widespread. Two panels hang in the Town House, Biggar, Lanarkshire, and are the work of a local tailor, Menzies Moffat (1829–1907). He was also a photographer, and took *carte de visite* portraits of local people. He was an eccentric and a recluse, regarded as something of a joke by his fellow townsmen, and tormented by the local small boys. He never married. *The Royal Crimean Hero Tablecloth*, named after a well-known pattern of table linen woven at Dunfermline, has a centrepiece with medallions of Queen Victoria and Prince Albert, surrounded by ladies of the court. There are figures from no less than 81 popular prints: Crimean leaders such as Lord Raglan, Omar Pasha and Maréchal Pelissier, as well as theatrical characters such as 'Mr. Payne as Robin Hood' and 'Mr. King as Little John' from Redington prints. There are narrow borders of contrasting material embroidered with flowers, stars and arabesques in silk using stitches employed by tailors: herringbone, buttonhole, backstitch and interlaced running stitch.

His second cover, an octagonal panel, *The Star*, is even more detailed and ambitious, and shows pictorial scenes, such as 'The Farmer's Farewell to his Grey' and 'Tam o' Shanter' as well as a portrait of the local medical practitioner, Dr Pairman, who died in 1870. Moffat wrote the story of his life in a

92. *Panel:* The Royal Clothograph Work of Art. *Inlaid patchwork of woollen material (probably tailors' clippings), inscribed 'John Monro the Paisley Artist-Tailor. Born May 16 1811. Author of the* Royal Clothograph Work of Art. *This Piece of Art took 18 years to complete at Odd Hours'. The designs are taken from popular prints. See Fig. 93.* (The Art Gallery and Museum, Kelvingrove, Glasgow)

A Pourtrait of Cook

M.ʳ T.P. COOKE as WILLIAM in BLACK EY'D SUSAN.

To the Manager and Gentlemen of the Surrey Theatre this Plate is respectfully dedicated by their Obedient and Humble Servant.

N.°27.

Pub. by M.& M. SKELT 11 Swan S.ᵗ Minorie London.

R. Lloyd. del. et Sc.

wallpaper pattern book, but that was destroyed. The *Tablecover* has only survived by accident. It was Moffat's last wish that he should be buried in it, but this was denied him, no doubt because it was considered eccentric and unseemly for one buried by the parish.

A tailor in Falkirk, David Robertson, also completed two covers, now in the Kelvingrove Museum, Glasgow. One, dated 1853, is inscribed 'Executed by David Robertson Falkirk Stirlingshire N B in 1650 hours'. It shows the royal arms and a fully rigged ship surrounded by figures from the 'tinsel prints' of generals and actors.

Even more detailed is *The Royal Clothograph Work of Art* (fig. 92) with its long inscription:

John Monro the Paisley Artist-Tailor. Born May 16 1811. Author of the Royal Clothograph Work of Art. This piece of Art took 18 years to complete at Odd Hours. All Round the Border is the Nems of Men of Learning and Genius, Some before Christ. To Gain the Grand End, We Ought to Keep in Mind 7 Words. 1st Push. 2nd Piety. 3rd Patience. 4th Perseverance 5th Punctuality. 6th Penetrate. 7th Please. Stop. Man know thyself And Others Learn to Know. Love GOD and Man Amen.

Depicted are three ships, a lion labelled 'Burns' and three theatrical scenes, one showing the well-known actor T.P. Cooke as William, his most famous role in the play *Black Ey'd Susan* by Jerrold. (Fig. 93.) *The Royal Clothograph* was valued at £150 and offered at a subscription sale (raffle) in March 1888 in Glasgow on behalf of Monro's widow.

Popular prints provided the models for these

93. *Theatrical print published by M. & M. Skelt, London, about 1830: T.P. Cooke as William in* Black Ey'd Susan, *a play by Douglas Jerrold. Cooke made his name as William at the Surrey Theatre in June 1829, when he played the part for a hundred performances. He repeated it many times at Covent Garden and the Adelphi Theatre. This print was used as a design for the panel labelled 'Britain for Ever' on Monro's Clothograph. (The Museum of London)*

remarkable patchwork panels. As we have seen, this was no new departure. Printed sources had been used as pattern designs since the time of Mary, Queen of Scots, whose embroiderer copied birds and animals from books of natural history, just as a book of engravings, published in London in 1630, provided the motifs worked by Grisell and Rachel Baillie in 1706, on the panel now at Mellerstain. Moreover, the pictorial scenes on these patchwork panels are pleasingly balanced, however disparate their subject matter now appears to us, and the borders are carefully chosen to set them off.

From the time of the Great Exhibition of 1851 there had been an increasing awareness of the importance of good design, though there was by no means universal agreement as to what constituted a 'good' design. As long ago as 1760, the Scottish Board of Trustees set up their Academy in Edinburgh with just such an object in mind, and it had been followed by government Schools of Design in different areas of Britain in succeeding decades. The opening of the Victoria & Albert Museum in London, followed by the Royal Scottish Museum (now part of the Royal Museum of Scotland) in 1854, with the intention of improving public taste, particularly in manufactures, was succeeded by the Royal School of Art Needlework in 1872. Other schools of needlework were established, not only to provide good designs, but also to offer employment to women and girls, who undertook well-designed work on commission. One, still in existence, is the Wemyss School of Needlework in Fife, founded by Miss Wemyss, later Lady Henry Grosvenor,[5] in 1877, to give employment in the mining village of Coaltown of Wemyss. At first specializing in whitework, especially layettes and trousseaux (fig. 94), the school, under Mrs Webster, the first Mistress, also undertook large pieces: curtains, banners and embroidered gowns, some of which were shown at the International Exhibition of Industry, Art and Science in Edinburgh in 1886, and the Chicago Exposition of 1893. Smocking and quilting, church work and chair covers were worked to order. Canvases were drawn to fit

94. Monogram 'Angela' *within a medallion. Fine
white satin stitch and beading on a sheer cambric
clothes cover. Worked by the Wemyss School of
Needlework in Fife, probably as part of a trousseau
about 1900. At first, the School specialized in
trousseaux and layettes. (*The Wemyss School of
Needlework*)*

95. *Lap quilt of cream satin, quilted in red back
stitch. Lined with white imitation fur powdered with
ermine tails. The Wemyss School was noted for its
quilting. Worked by Lady Victoria Wemyss about
1935. (Lady Victoria Wemyss)*

individual chairs and settees for the owners to work themselves in the traditional way. Lady Henry Grosvenor was an accomplished artist, and the designs were of high quality. The School continues today, though reduced in staff, under the direction of Lady Victoria Wemyss, herself a notable needlewoman, who has added greatly to the collection of designs, mostly from antique sources, that the School holds. (Fig. 95.)

Lady Henry Grosvenor received no formal training as an artist. A contemporary living in Edinburgh was able to exercise her talent with much greater fulfilment as an artist. She was Phoebe Traquair (Phoebe Anna Moss, 1852–1936). Born in Dublin, she trained at the art classes organized by the Royal Dublin Society, and in 1873 married Dr Ramsay Traquair, Keeper of the Department of Natural History, the Royal Scottish Museum. By the mid-1880s she had begun manuscript illumination, in addition to embroidery, and later undertook tooled bookbindings and enamelling. In 1885 she received her first commission for mural decoration, for the Royal Edinburgh Sick Children's Hospital, to be followed by one for the Song School of St Mary's Cathedral (1888–92). A third for the Catholic Apostolic Church, also in Edinburgh, was executed between 1893 and 1900.

A prolific and versatile artist, she continued to embroider during all these years. She exhibited widely, in Chicago, St Louis and Paris as well as London and Edinburgh. She was one of the few Scottish members of the Arts and Crafts Society and the Guild of Women Bookbinders. Her embroidery glows with colour, with a wide palette of silks and laid gold, used with superlative technique. Four large panels, symbolic of the four stages in the spiritual life of man, show *The*

96. Panel: The Entrance. *One of a set of four panels worked by Phoebe Traquair, depicting stages in man's spiritual life. Surface and laid stitches in silks and gold on linen. Phoebe Traquair was a painter of murals, a bookbinder and enameller as well as an embroiderer. 1895. 223.5 × 91.5 cm/88 × 36 in. (The National Gallery of Scotland)*

Entrance: a red-haired youth with lyre, against a background of vines. (Fig. 96.) This is followed by *The Stress* and *Despair*, where, his lyre broken, he hangs from a tree encircled by a serpent, and *Victory*, where a seraph rescues him in an embrace from the serpent's jaws. These enigmatic and richly patterned panels were completed between 1885 and 1902, and were considered by the artist to be her best work.[6]

References

1. But see B. Morris, *Victorian Embroidery*, Herbert Jenkins, 1962, for a serious appraisal of the period.
2. RSM, 1942.41. It is 5 ft 7 ins by 7 ft.
3. I am indebted to Mr Richard E. Early for his kindness in supplying this information.
4. It is often called 'inlaid appliqué'. See Caulfeild and Saward's *Dictionary of Needlework* (1882).
5. Miss Dora Wemyss married Lord Henry Grosvenor in 1887. She was also the patron of the Wemyss Pottery, Kirkcaldy, to which she contributed designs, as well as helping it to get recognition in London. She died in 1894.
6. I am indebted to Elizabeth Cummings (Mrs Murray Simpson) for kindly supplying this information about Phoebe Traquair, the subject of her forthcoming doctoral thesis.

CHAPTER TEN

The Glasgow School of Art

In 1894 a radical change in the teaching of embroidery began in Glasgow. It started modestly enough. Mrs Newbery, the wife of the Principal of the Glasgow School of Art, initiated and conducted an embroidery class for full-time students of the School, extending it to anyone interested in the new embroidery. Jessie Newbery, née Rowat (1864–1948) (fig. 97) had a profoundly independent outlook. Born into a family involved in textiles – her father was a manufacturer of Paisley shawls and other relatives were engaged in the sewed muslin industry – she became a full-time student at the Glasgow School of Art, going through the Life School for drawing and anatomy, and taking the Design course in stained glass and textiles. In 1889 she married the Principal, Francis H. Newbery (1853–1946), whose energy and enthusiasm encouraged the talents of all his students. These included 'the Four': Charles Rennie Mackintosh and his wife Margaret Macdonald, and her younger sister Frances, who married Herbert McNair, a fellow student with Mackintosh, who was later to teach at the School of Architecture in Liverpool.

Mrs Newbery's approach to embroidery was individual and direct. Unlike the Royal School of Needlework in London, whose teaching, like that of William Morris, was firmly based on examples from the past, she believed it should reflect, and indeed be an integral part of, the new artistic movement that was erupting with astonishing vitality in the School of Art. She wrote no books, but was persuaded in 1898 to set down her beliefs as an artist: 'I believe in education consisting of seeing the best that has been done. Then, having this high standard thus set before us, in doing what we like to do: *that* for our fathers, *this* for us . . . I believe that . . . the design and decoration of a pepper pot is as important, in its degree, as the conception of a cathedral.'[1]

She impressed her ideas upon her students, so that a recognizable Glasgow style of embroidery evolved. At first she followed the Morris tradition, using coloured crewels on linen, but soon began to develop a characteristic linen appliqué with simple stylized flowers and leaves cut out of coloured linens and outlined with satin stitch in silk, usually Pearsall's Mallard Floss. (Fig. 98.) The stems coiled in strong lines, emphasizing the shape of the article. Her designs, and those of her students, are now loosely labelled 'Art Nouveau', but her daughter has pointed out that the Newberys and the Mackintoshes thoroughly disliked the continental Art Nouveau and thought they were working to counter it.[2] 'I like the opposition of straight lines to curved; of horizontal to vertical . . . I specially aim at beautifully shaped spaces and try to make them as important as the patterns,' she wrote. The embroidery on household furnishings and linens was an integral part of a simple interior, not an added distraction. Light, short casement curtains, often with embroidered hem, began to replace the heavy dark chenille curtains in households interested in the new artistic movement.

An uncle took her for a month's visit to Italy at the age of eighteen. She became entranced by the primitive painters, by the mosaics of Ravenna and Rome, and by the peasant crafts, especially the textiles and pottery. She initiated from them the technique of needleweaving whereby threads are

97. Mrs Newbery (Jessie Rowat, 1864–1948), wife of the Principal of the Glasgow School of Art, who started embroidery classes for the students and others in 1894. She designed and made her own clothes.

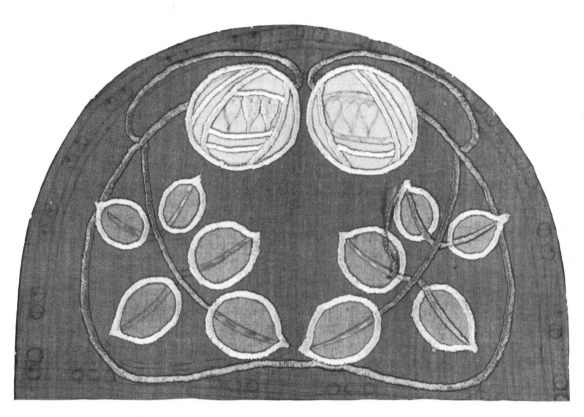

98. *Tea-cosy (unfinished) designed and worked by Jessie Newbery. Blue linen with pink and green linen appliqué outlined in silk satin stitch. Mrs Newbery is said to have originated the characteristic 'Glasgow Rose' with circles of linen, cut out freehand, the folded petals indicated by lines of satin stitch.*
29.5 × 40.8 cm/11½ × 16 in. (Mary Newbery Sturrock)

withdrawn from handwoven linen and geometrical borders made by darning or whipping the exposed threads with coloured yarn. (Fig. 99.)

Mrs Newbery's clothes reflected her independent outlook. Although not a follower of the 'aesthetic' nor even the 'rational' dress movement, she disliked tight corseting and the unnatural shape it produced. She never wore a corset – she had no need, as she was small and slim. She designed and made her own clothes in soft, warm lightweight materials, with gathered skirt held in by an embroidered belt, full sleeves and embroi-

dered collar or yoke, the neck filled in with a delicate frill of white net drawn up with narrow velvet ribbon. Later in life, she simplified her dress still further. A garment worn in the 1930s, over light warm underwear and a long skirt, is a simple magyar shape. The neck is decorated with felt appliqué and the seams joined by a brightly coloured faggot stitch. Another, of black velvet, has a neck opening emphasized by appliqué edged with a handmade woollen cord and is fastened with metal Russian clasps. She also designed and made the dresses worn by her two small daughters, Elsie and Mary.[3] (Fig. 100.)

In her embroidery class, the cut and decoration of clothes was taught, with the aim that the garments should be both practical and beautiful. Mrs Newbery's personal style made its impact, and her students all developed an individual attitude to dress, including Ann Macbeth (1875–1948) (fig. 101) who, while still a student, became

99. *Cushion cover, designed and worked by Jessie Newbery. Unbleached linen embroidered in coloured crewel wools using satin, long-and-short and stem stitches, with a border of needleweaving. The inscription reads, 'Under every grief and pine Runs a joy with silken twine'. Mrs Newbery was exceedingly interested in lettering and introduced it into many of her embroideries. 1900. 55.8 × 48.8 cm/22 × 19¼ in. (Glasgow Museum and Art Gallery E1953.53c)*

ENTWÜRFE FÜR KINDERKLEIDCHEN VON R. JESSIE NEWBERY GLASGOW.

100. *Illustration from* Moderne Stickerein, *published by Alex Koch, Darmstadt 1905. Design for children's clothes by Jessie Newbery, Glasgow. The designs for embroidery, lace and interior design included those by Jessie M. King, Margaret Mackintosh, Leni Matthaei and M. Baillie Scott. (Mary Newbery Sturrock)*

Assistant Instructress to Mrs Newbery in 1901, and then succeeded her as head of the department in 1908, when Mrs Newbery retired owing to illness.

Ann Macbeth, granddaughter of Norman Macbeth RSA and the daughter of an engineer, entered the School in 1897 and brought the fervour of an apostle to Mrs Newbery's teaching. Although she also taught metalwork and bookbinding, she is

101. *Ann Macbeth (1875–1948) who became Assistant Instructress to Mrs Newbery in 1901 and succeeded her in 1908. The wide embroidered collar, evolved by Mrs Newbery, was adopted by many of her students. Note the circular 'Glasgow Rose' and stylized leaves. (Photo by Annan, Glasgow)*

best remembered for her pioneering approach to the teaching of needlework in schools. A Saturday morning class for teachers had been initiated, at which Fra Newbery himself taught, in order that a new direction should be given to the teaching of arts and crafts to schoolchildren. Ann Macbeth and her assistant, Margaret Swanson, taught the needlework. In 1911 they published *Educational Needlecraft*, formulating an entirely new method of needlework education.

In place of the fine hemming and the cross stitch sampler (still being produced in Scottish schools) the child was from the first encouraged to develop colour sense by using tacking stitches in coloured thread, starting with a knot. A rectangle of calico, its hem held down with these running stitches, could be made into a table mat. Folded, it could become a bag, drawn up by a handmade cord, which two children, twisting in opposite directions, could make themselves. Each lesson resulted in a finished article, with construction and decoration dependent on each other. The joining of seams was part of the decoration of a garment. Coloured darning was first introduced to strengthen and decorate a flannel needlecase; only later was it used to repair a hole. Household linens were embellished with straight lines, squares or circles, and later with coloured appliqué or needleweaving.

So much of this is taken for granted today that we are apt to forget how revolutionary it was in 1911. Ann Macbeth was intensely practical, and though we may smile at some of the garments – the combinations with their knee-level frills, for instance – the book deserves re-reading, for it was a milestone in the teaching of needlework.[4] By the end of the course, the pupil had learned the rudiments of plain sewing, garment construction and embroidery. The syllabus was probably contributed by Margaret Swanson, herself a schoolteacher.

It was not only schoolchildren whom Ann Macbeth sought to convert. A prolific worker herself, undertaking many large commissions, she designed embroideries for Liberty, and other woven fabrics for Donald Brothers of Dundee. Her

enthusiasm persuaded her friends, and especially members of the Women's Institute, that they could undertake large pieces and even make their own designs, however simple. She retired to Patterdale in the Lake District. There she lectured to Women's Institutes, taught rug making (using the fleece of the native Herdwick sheep), painted christening mugs for the children baptized in the dale, and worked several hangings and a Lenten frontal for the parish church. (Fig. 102.)

Many other graduates of the Glasgow School became noted for their embroidery. Frances Macdonald assisted Mrs Newbery in her embroidery classes. Her sister Margaret developed her characteristic style of embroidery as an integral part of the decoration of the interiors designed by her architect husband, Charles Rennie Mackintosh, whom she married in 1900. (Colour plate IX) One of their first ventures was the set of panels she embroidered for the room designed by her husband for the Turin exhibition of 1902, an exhibition that did much to enhance the reputation of the Glasgow School of Art, and to which Mrs Newbery and Ann Macbeth also contributed.

Indeed, the School of Art under Fra Newbery, who retired in 1918, must be regarded as the source of present day attitudes to embroidery. It was Fra Newbery, an admirer of William Morris, who promoted it from being a minor craft to a department of the Art School. It was Mrs Newbery's refreshing vision: '. . . *that* for our fathers, *this* for us . . .' that encouraged the full-time students to apply their talents for design to a medium that they might have despised. It was Ann Macbeth who with her practical approach and burning enthusiasm widened the choice open to the amateur, encouraging her to use simpler designs of her own devising, instead of being dependent on iron-on transfers.[5]

Before she retired from Glasgow in 1928, Ann Macbeth had been assisted by Anne Knox Arthur, who succeeded her.[6] She was followed in 1932 by Kathleen Mann ARCA, who had been a student of Rebecca Crompton. Her style, spare and linear, was dependent on good draughtsmanship.[7] (Fig.

102. *Panel:* The Nativity, *Designed and worked by Ann Macbeth. Surface stitches in coloured wools on natural linen. Set in the village of Patterdale, Cumbria, where Ann Macbeth worked the panel, with Helvellyn in the background. The angel holds a Star of Bethlehem; the other flowers are associated with the Virgin: Marigold, Lady's Smock and Lady's Slipper.* 1940. 75 × 78.5 *cm*/46½ × 55¾ *in.* (Glasgow Museum and Art Gallery E1946.25)

103.) Kathleen Mann was succeeded after only four years by Agnes McCredie, who, influenced by developments in Scandinavia, added weaving to the curriculum. She managed to maintain the department of Embroidery and Weaving through the rigours and shortages of the Second World War.

A new and richly creative period began with the appointment of Kathleen Whyte as head of the

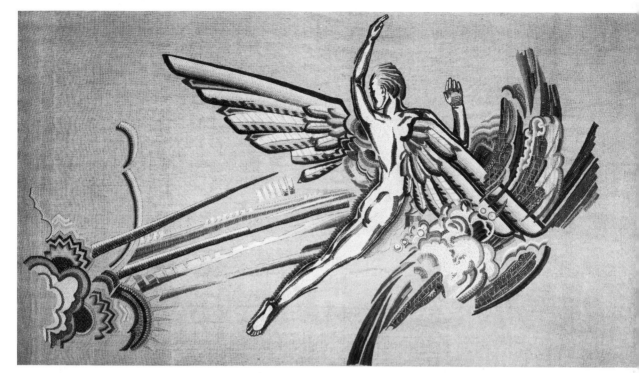

department in 1948. She was not a student of the Glasgow School of Art; indeed, she brought with her, in addition to her immense enthusiasm for embroidery and colour, a totally different tradition. Born in Arbroath, and like Ann Macbeth, the child of an engineer, she inherited his talent for draughtsmanship. Part of her childhood had been spent in India. She became intoxicated by colour and learned to appreciate fine fabrics. Back in Scotland she studied at Gray's School of Art in Aberdeen, specializing in embroidery under Dorothy Angus. (Fig. 104.) Dorothy Angus had been a student at Edinburgh under Louisa Chart. Unlike Mrs Newbery and Ann Macbeth, who had both used a comparatively limited repertoire of stitches

104. Wall hanging: Icarus, *designed and worked by Kathleen Whyte as a Diploma piece at Gray's School of Art, Aberdeen 1932. The cartoon was drawn in charcoal on white paper in the Design department under James Hamilton and later interpreted in stitchery in the Embroidery department under Dorothy Angus. (Trustees of the Royal Museum of Scotland 1977.145)*

to obtain their effects, Louisa Chart and Dorothy Angus believed that stitchery was the basis of embroidery, and revelled in the variety of textures it offered. In the same way in the past, Mary, Queen of Scots had limited herself to cross and tent stitch, without sharing the enthusiasm for complicated stitches that seized the Elizabethan Englishwoman. Kathleen Whyte, therefore, taught and explored the possibilities of the vast resources of stitches available to the embroiderer, experimenting, after the dearth of materials during the war, with yarns and fabrics unimagined in the past, but all controlled by rigorous draughtsmanship. She has been a persuasive teacher, with a dazzling gift

103. Panel by Kathleen Mann: The Little Visitor. *Appliqué of gingham, silk, braids and lace, with surface stitching on open canvas. It was used as frontispiece to her book* Appliqué Design and Method, *1937. (Glasgow Museum and Art Gallery E1946.88)*

147

for words.[8] She drew out, and respected, the individual talent of each of her students, so that, under her, there was no recognizable 'Glasgow style' as there was at the time of Mrs Newbery and Ann Macbeth. Just as they did, she has widened the concept of embroidery. Her students, in this country and abroad, are still exploring, and have not yet found, the boundaries of embroidery. Her greatest achievement has been to give back to the embroiderer the status of an artist: one who works in textile fibres rather than in paint, stone or metal.

She has undertaken many commissions, and estimates that she and her students have supplied more than fifty churches in Scotland with pulpit falls. (See appendix.) For the Queen Mother Maternity Hospital in Glasgow a large panel, six feet by two feet, titled *Storks flying in the Dawn*, was commissioned as a token of gratitude by a young architect. When HM Queen Elizabeth the Queen Mother opened the road bridge over the River Tay, Kathleen Whyte made a delicate stole to be presented to Her Majesty. It is in handwoven pure silk in cream and gold, incorporating the symbols of Angus, Dundee and Fife, embellished with forty mussel pearls from the river itself. Mayfield Church in Edinburgh, partly destroyed by fire in 1968, commissioned a cloth to cover the new Communion table of plain wood. (Colour plate X.) It shows the Hand of God (a symbol used in early Bible illustrations) with wing-like shapes, suggesting banners, converging on it in a great arc, in appliqué of silks and rayons in more than sixty shades.

In 1956 Kathleen Whyte initiated the Glasgow School of Art Embroidery (now the Embroidery/ Textile) Group, which holds an exhibition every

second year of the work of former students and staff. (Fig. 105.) This offers a useful focus for commissions and a powerful stimulus to amateur embroiderers.

She retired from the School in 1974 to be succeeded by one of her own students, Crissie White, who trained 1956–60, and had previously held the post of Lecturer in Embroidery and Woven Textiles at the Duncan of Jordanstone College of Art, Dundee. Under her leadership, the boundaries of embroidery have exploded in experimental techniques that no longer confine themselves to textile fibres or woven grounds. (Fig. 106.)

Crissie White has also undertaken many commissions. The most striking is perhaps the silk hanging *Joseph's Coat* for the Department of Surgical Neurology, Dundee Royal Infirmary. She has designed and worked a stole for the Moderator of the General Assembly of the Church of Scotland, the Revd John Paterson, St Luke's Church, Milngavie, and has undertaken pulpit falls for many churches. One, for New Kilpatrick Parish Church of Scotland, Bearsden, is intended for use during Lent. It is worked in pale mauve, rather than the traditional purple, which in certain lights can look black, and symbolizes hope rising from despair. (Fig. 107.) A simple, strongly controlled design shows the Cross in concentric circles of the red and mauve of pain and sorrow rising to the golden shades of hope. They are rayed by the blood-tipped crown of thorns. Above rises the Dove of the Spirit and of hope.

Until the 1970s, the Diploma course at the Glasgow School of Art, under the very rigorous standards of the Scottish Education Department, entailed two years of general art education in drawing, painting, sculpture, architecture, graphic and textile design, together with the history of art and architecture and a choice of craft. This was followed by two years of specialization in, for instance, the department of Embroidery and Weaving. In 1978 the School's art and design courses were validated by the Council of National Academic Awards: the Diploma of Art is no longer

105. Pulpit fall, representing the Fish, an early Christian symbol, designed and worked by Marilyn McGregor, 1979. Appliqué of silver lamé, embroidered in silk and cord with Celtic motifs, and Greek letters symbolizing 'Jesus Christ, Son of God the Saviour' on a background of turquoise-blue dupion silk. 53.5 × 48 cm/21 × 33 in. (Marilyn McGregor)

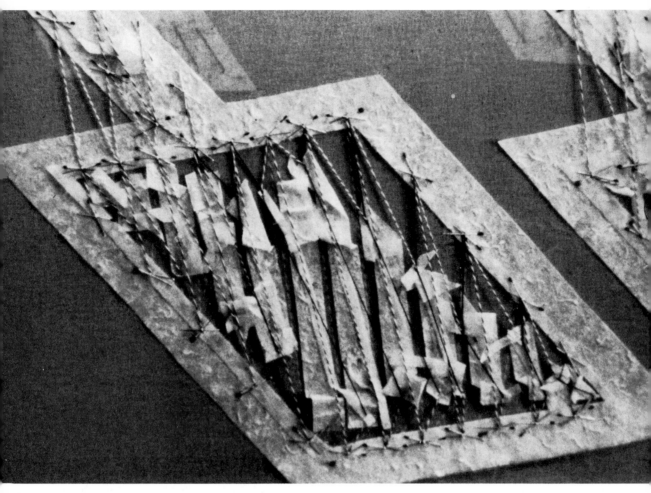

106. *Panel designed and worked by Ian Black who graduated from the Glasgow School of Art in 1980. Embroidery on organdie using handmade paper, pins and thread, the design based on an aerial view of airfields (detail).* (Ian Black)

107. *Lenten pulpit fall, designed and worked by Crissie White, Head of the Department of Embroidered and Woven Textiles, Glasgow School of Art, for New Kilpatrick Parish Church, Bearsden.*

The theme symbolizes hope rising out of despair. A cross surrounded by a crown of thorns, surmounted by a rising dove, on a pale mauve background. Colour is skilfully used to reinforce the symbolism. The points of some of the thorns are red; the concentric circles, mauve and red below, shade to a golden hue above to suggest hope. The design is mounted on hardboard and heavily padded, the cross of balsa wood covered with leather and silk. 1980. (Crissie White)

awarded, its place taken by the BA and BA (Hons) degrees. This was followed by the other Scottish art colleges. Glasgow remains, however, the only college to have a department entitled 'Embroidery and Weaving'. At the other art colleges, although embroidery may still be offered as a subsidiary subject, the word no longer features in the titles of the departments of textile design.

References

An invaluable source of reference to the early days of the School is the exhibition catalogue: *Glasgow School of Art Embroidery 1894–1920* by Fiona C. Macfarlane and Elizabeth F. Arthur. Glasgow Museums and Art Galleries, 1980.

1. *Studio* Vol. 12, 1898, pp. 47–51.
2. I am indebted to her daughter, Mary Newbery Sturrock, for this information. Mary Sturrock followed her mother in becoming an accomplished artist. In 1915 she won the annual prize for embroidery at the School of Art. Although she specialized as a potter and flower painter, she has always been an embroiderer and like her mother, designs and makes her own clothes.
3. M. Swain, 'Mrs J.R. Newbery, 1864–1948'. *Embroidery* Winter 1973, p. 106. 'Mrs Newbery's Dress', *Costume* 24, 1978, pp. 64–73.
4. Margaret Swanson attended the third course of the teachers' certificate in 1905. She was Assistant Instructress with Ann Macbeth from 1910–13. Publications: *Needlecraft in the School*, London, 1919. *Needlecraft for older girls*, London, 1920. *Needlecraft and psychology*, London, 1926.
5. Other publications by Ann Macbeth: *The Playwork Book*, Methuen, 1918. *School and Fireside Crafts* (with May Spence), Methuen, 1920. *Embroidered Lace and Leatherwork*, 1924. *Needleweaving*, Simpson, Kendal, 1926. *The Countrywoman's Rug Book*, Dryad, Leicester, 1929.
   See also M. Swain, 'Ann Macbeth', *Embroidery* 25 no.1, 1974, p. 9.
6. Anne Knox Arthur published *An Embroidery Book*, A. & C. Black, 1920, reprinted 1931. The designs are still largely influenced by Ann Macbeth.
7. Publications: K. Mann, *Peasant Costume in Europe* Books I and II, A. & C. Black, 1931, reprinted 1935 and 1937. *Embroidery Design and Stitches*, A. & C. Black, 1937. *Appliqué Design and Method*, A. & C. Black, 1937.
8. Kathleen Whyte was made a Member of the Order of the British Empire in 1969 for services to education in Scotland. Publications: *Design in Embroidery*, Batsford, 1969. 'Warp and Weft – a personal account', *Embroidery* 26 no. 1, Spring 1975, pp. 8–25.

CHAPTER ELEVEN

Talented Amateurs

Many accomplished needlewomen, particularly at the beginning of this century, remained indifferent to the persuasive teaching of Mrs Newbery and Ann Macbeth at the Glasgow School of Art. The Glasgow designs were regarded as 'Art Nouveau' and unsuitable for ancient houses, especially those embellished with needlework from the past. Indeed, Art Nouveau did not become an aristocratic taste, but was rather the choice of the middle-class intellectual. Moreover, it was obviously unsuitable when replacing the covers of eighteenth-century chairs. When one or two canvas work covers from a large set became worn or damaged, it was customary to have the design copied on to new canvas for the worn chairs. The replacements would be worked as closely as possible to the original in order to keep the set intact. The Royal School of Needlework in London and the Wemyss School in Fife, became adept at the faithful rendering of an old chair cover to match the rest of the set.

This was the course followed at the palace of Holyroodhouse by HM Queen Mary, when the worn covers of some of the chairs that had originally belonged to Lord Adam Gordon[1] were re-drawn on to new canvas by the Royal School of Needlework in London and worked by the ladies of Scotland. Additional canvases were drawn, duplicating some of the designs, of classical figures or card players, for instance, in order to cover additional chairs with slightly different legs, thus making a large matching set for the State Drawing Rooms.

Since canvas work is one of the most durable of upholstery fabrics, other owners have continued in the tradition of their ancestors, making covers for individual chairs and settees, or even whole sets, and selecting a traditional pattern to harmonize with the age of the chair.

The colours chosen were usually muted, sometimes to match the rest of the set, but also in the mistaken belief that the vegetable dyes used in the past resulted in soft shades. It is often forgotten that the canvas work of the past that we now see has faded over the years from the intense, almost strident colours that were first used. Examination of the underside of early chair covers reveals that our ancestors had a taste for brilliant colour that we would now judge quite out of character with a traditional interior.

Owners of four-poster beds, whose hangings were notoriously subject to hard wear, when curtains were continually being drawn and bed covers removed nightly, wished to renew them in a suitable style. Sometimes the almost indestructible crewel work was cut out and re-mounted on to a new linen twill: a daunting task, but one frequently undertaken by the patient amateur. Otherwise, sympathetic new curtains had to be devised, a very satisfying undertaking for the enthusiasm and skill of the devoted needlewoman. A pelmet and bedhead at Glamis Castle was worked by Cecilia, Countess of Strathmore and Kinghorne, who died in 1938. She was the mother of HM Queen Elizabeth, the Queen Mother. Worked in silk, the padded bedhead in a gilt frame has a design of thistles and roses, with a coroneted S cipher. The inner pelmet, hidden at first glance, is richly embroidered and bears the Strathmore arms, with the initials of the Countess's ten children around

the sides. (Fig. 108.) For another bed, belonging to her daughter, Lady Elphinstone, she embroidered on fawn satin a tester, valance, bedhead, bedspread and pillow. (Fig. 109.)

Another prolific needlewoman was Constance, wife of the twenty-seventh Earl of Crawford and Balcarres. She died in 1947. No less than ten large bed covers, worked by her in a variety of techniques, remain at Balcarres.[2] One, adapted from a blackwork pillow cover that belonged to Lord Falkland[3] has the initials of her children and family (Lindsay) mottoes on the meandering leaves. (Fig.

109. Cushion embroidered by Cecilia, Countess of Strathmore, part of a set of embroidered bed furnishings, consisting of tester, valance, bedhead, bedspread and cushion all worked by her. She married in 1881 and died in 1938. Coloured silks on fawn satin; satin stitch and stem stitch; chenille fringe. (Lord Elphinstone)

110.) Her daughter-in-law, Mary, Countess of Crawford, has continued the tradition, and a set of eleven chairs bear covers worked by her. Indeed, in many Scottish houses with a store of historic needlework, the tradition of the past has been carried on by the present owners, who add their own contribution to the needlework furnishings.

At Traquair, Flora, wife of Peter Maxwell Stuart, has added chair covers in Florentine stitch to the store of embroideries to be seen in the house. Two carpets completed by Mary, Countess of Dalhousie (fig. 111) remind one of the unfinished

108. Bed at Glamis Castle, with bedhead and pelmet embroidered by Cecilia, Countess of Strathmore, mother of HM Queen Elizabeth, the Queen Mother. Around the inner pelmet she embroidered the initials of her children. Coloured silks on cream satin. (The Earl and Countess of Strathmore and Kinghorne)

110. *Bed cover worked by Constance, Countess of Crawford and Balcarres. The leaves, in a variety of stitches and fillings, bear the initials of her children, and family mottoes. Coloured wools, chiefly greens, on linen, c. 1914. (Mary, Countess of Crawford and Balcarres)*

carpet made by the mother and sisters of the tenth Earl.[4] At Wemyss Castle, already graced by the enchanting bed curtains embroidered in 1727 to 1730 (see colour plate II), Lady Victoria Wemyss has worked bed covers, several sets of chair covers and many carpets. Since her marriage to Captain Michael Wemyss in 1918, when she took charge of the Wemyss School of Needlework, she has embroidered continuously. Her taste and expertise has had a profound influence on much of the canvas work done for the home in Scotland.

Men have also added their contribution to embroidered furnishings. The Earl of Haddington, descended from Lady Grisell Baillie whose two daughters made the panel of 1706 now at Mellerstain, has made chair covers and needlework pictures for Tyninghame.

The most outstanding contribution to a house filled with the needlework of her ancestors must surely be the exquisite whitework panel of the British Royal Arms (fig. 112) at Blair Castle, made by Lady Evelyn Stuart Murray (1868–1940) daughter of the seventh Duke of Atholl. This is of such high quality that one would be tempted to describe it as professional work if its background were not known. Delicate and painfully shy, she took refuge in embroidery. Her mother engaged a teacher, and she spent some years in Belgium where she studied the exacting technique of Brussels *point de gaze*.

III. Carpet (detail): Waterbirds and Fish, *designed and worked by Mary, Countess of Dalhousie, who died in 1960. Wool cross stitch on canvas. 1920s.* (The Earl of Dalhousie)

For her masterpiece (as it may truthfully be described) she adapted this technique, using a ground of sheer woven cambric instead of the delicate needlemade mesh of the Brussels lace. The trial pieces for her remarkable panel are preserved at Blair Castle, where she grew up, together with samplers of other varieties of embroidery that she mastered with consummate skill. Each one is worked with precision, using the finest of materials and threads. Little is known of her life or of her teachers. All that is remembered is that at the end of her long life, sadly, she lost her sight.

It is entirely fitting that her panel, one of the finest pieces of Scottish embroidery of this century, should owe its origin and technique to the Low Countries, whence came the inspiration for the early pieces, such as the Fetternear Banner.

112. Panel: The British Royal Arms, *worked by Lady Evelyn Stuart Murray (1868–1940). The arms are enclosed in a scrolled border, decorated with roses, thistles and shamrocks and the Prince of Wales's feathers with the motto* Ich dien. *White cotton on fine cambric,* c.1912. 55.8 × 65.3 cm/22 × 25 in. *(The Duke of Atholl)*

Charles Rennie Mackintosh and his wife Margaret Macdonald had believed, like William Morris, that embroidery ought to play an important part in the interior decoration of a house. Another, and more immediately successful architect than Mackintosh, Sir Robert Lorimer, RSA (1864–1929), built distinctive houses and reconstructed many ancient mansions in Scotland, as well as designing the Scottish War Memorial on the rock of Edinburgh Castle. In addition to stonework,

furniture and ironwork, his designs included needlework which the amateur could undertake to complete the interior. A dedicated collector of tapestries and needlework, with a discerning eye, he designed, among other pieces, two large bedcovers for his own home, Kellie Castle, Fife. His sister, Louise Lorimer, a gifted artist, is shown in a painting by John, their brother, seated in a window embroidering a bedcover. One (figs. 113 and 114) worked in coloured silks on linen, was embroidered by Mrs Jeannie Skinner, the postmistress at Arncrosh, under the direction of Louise. It was designed for the Vine Room, a bedroom with a handsome plaster ceiling at Kellie Castle.

An artist who contributed embroidery of high quality to her own home, which was designed by her architect husband, was Maggie Hamilton (1867–1952). (Fig. 115.) The sister of J. Whitelaw

113. *Sketch, ink and watercolour on paper by Sir Robert Lorimer, RSA, ARA. Design for a bed cover for the Vine Room, Kellie Castle.* (The Royal Commission on the Ancient and Historical Monuments of Scotland)

Hamilton, RSA she was at the centre of the distinguished group of painters working at Glasgow at that time. A talented artist herself, she appears to have received no formal training. In 1883–5 she stayed at Cockburnspath, where the Glasgow school of painters congregated, with the mother of James Guthrie (later Sir James Guthrie PRSA, 1854–1932, who painted her several times). In 1897 she married the architect Alexander N. Paterson, younger brother of James Paterson RSA.

115. Maggie Hamilton (Mrs A.N. Paterson 1867–1952) at her embroidery frame in her home, Long Croft, Helensburgh. A stained glass medallion of Embroidery can be seen in the window. ?1908. (Royal Commission on the Ancient and Historic Monuments of Scotland)

114. Detail of a bed cover made for Kellie Castle, designed by Sir Robert Lorimer. Worked by Mrs Skinner under the direction of Miss Louise Lorimer. Coloured wools on linen twill, c.1900. (The Trustees of the Royal Museum of Scotland)

Mrs Paterson designed and worked several panels to decorate the rooms of Long Croft, Helensburgh, designed by her husband as their own home in 1902. One, still in position, worked in silks and silver thread, is over the fireplace of the sitting room. Another, of cupids and stylized flowers, was removed from the dining room in 1947.[5] Over the fireplace of the hall is a painted panel, perhaps a cartoon for an embroidered one now in the Royal Museum of Scotland, of doves

116. *Panel:* Doves and Clematis, *designed and worked by Maggie Hamilton. Chinese silks on cream damask. A painted version of this design hangs over the fireplace of the hall at Long Croft. About 1900.* 61×182 *cm/*$24 \times 71\frac{1}{2}$ *in. (*The Trustees of the Royal Museum of Scotland*)*

and clematis worked in Chinese silks on cream damask. (Fig. 116.) She was twice Vice-President of the Lady Artists' Club of Glasgow, in 1928 and 1937, and exhibited paintings regularly. She was not entirely sympathetic to the work of Mrs Newbery and Ann Macbeth; as an embroiderer she had her own style, which owed more to the Arts and Crafts movement than to the Glasgow School of Art.

Over the past century, the Church of Scotland began to relax its long ban on decoration in the Kirk, and many dedicated amateurs were allowed to embroider pulpit falls and discreet pieces such as alms bags to relieve the often spartan interior of their parish church. Since Presbyterians sit to pray, this did not include kneelers. These are used in the Episcopal and Catholic churches, and have given embroiderers an opportunity to exercise their skills more widely in the service of the church. Kneeling pads, or hassocks, with canvas work

covers, require several workers to complete the set at the same time. If supplied by a single worker, the first would have become soiled and worn before the last was completed. It says much for the present day standard of skill that several ambitious projects have been undertaken by dedicated volunteers, all of whom have to submit to a test of competence before being allowed to join. Falkland Palace, a favourite hunting lodge of the Stuart kings and of Mary, Queen of Scots and her son James VI, still retains its ancient chapel, now used by the local Catholic congregation. The palace is in the care of the National Trust for Scotland. In 1980, 148 canvas work kneelers were dedicated, the work of volunteers. The kneelers were designed by the architect W. Schomberg Scott, himself an embroiderer, and display the thistle, the rose and the lily, symbols of Scotland, England and France, which appear on the painted ceiling of the chapel. (Fig. 117.)

On St Columba's island of Iona in the Hebrides, the Duke of Argyll in 1899 presented the ancient Abbey church to the Church of Scotland to be used for interdenominational worship. The church has now been restored and attracts many pilgrims each year. Over a period of six years, from 1963 to 1969, twenty-one stall cushions and forty-two kneelers

117. *Three kneelers made for the chapel at Falkland Palace, Fife. The motifs derive from the plasterwork of the ceiling. Designed by W. Schomberg Scott ARIBA, and worked by volunteers. The rose and thistle are yellow on a red ground, the fleur-de-lis on a green ground. Cross stitch on canvas. 1980. (The National Trust for Scotland)*

were made by volunteers all over Scotland, led by Lady (Rachel) Younger. They were designed by the artist Adam Robson. The kneelers are of four different designs; the stall cushions bear the symbols of the family of the Dukes of Argyll. (Fig. 118.)

Canvas work has always been the first choice of the amateur in Scotland since the time of Mary, Queen of Scots. It can be worked in the hand or on a frame, the design drawn on the canvas or counted from a chart. It can be used for small items, like the slips at Traquair and Scone, or for large hangings, valances, table carpets as at Arniston, or sets of durable chair covers. As we have seen, other

118. *Stall cushion made for the Abbey Church of Iona. The arms of the Duke of Argyll, chief of Clan Campbell, on a dark blue ground, surrounded by bog myrtle, the clan badge. Designed by Adam Robson and worked by Miss S.G.F Muirhead. 1969.* (The Abbey Church of Iona)

---

techniques have become fashionable from time to time. Jane Oliphant, Countess of Hopetoun, is depicted making a knotted net (see fig. 62) that was darned to produce the geometrical lace that Mary, Queen of Scots herself knew how to make. During the early part of this century, *lacis*, as this darned net was known (*filet brodé*), was revived in Scotland. This was due to the enthusiasm and scholarship of Mrs Simpson, who discovered and charted a great number of sixteenth-century patterns and published them under the pen name of 'Carita'.[6] She held classes in Edinburgh and was an inspiring if exacting teacher. Most students made their own net, of varying fineness according to the gauge used, but until the 1930s hand-knotted net could still be obtained from Italy. The darned rectangles were used as insets for white linen bedspreads and tablecloths. (Fig. 119.)

Ribbon work was a minor craft belonging more properly to the nineteenth century, when narrow ribbons, about 3 mm wide, sometimes parti-coloured, were used in a large-eyed needle and combined with silk embroidery to form flowers and other raised motifs. This very fragile embroidery was still being made until 1939 by one or two workshops, and sold by the Royal Repository for the Work of Indigent Gentlewomen in Edinburgh. (Fig. 120.) It decorated nightdress cases, handkerchief and glove sachets, and tea-cosies.

The Second World War of 1939–45 was a watershed that swept away many of the traditional techniques. Materials and threads for embroidery were unobtainable; fabric for clothing and furnishing was strictly rationed. When the war ended, tastes had changed. Patchwork, made as a thrifty substitute for scarce materials during the war, developed into an art form. This was partly owing to the enthusiasm of Edith Clark, one of the founders of the Scottish Handcraft Circle, set up in the 1950s to encourage all amateur crafts, but which has concentrated heavily on embroidery. Edith Clark's patchwork was meticulous, often using tiny patches, from which she made bags, boxes and cushions. Patchwork is now regarded as a separate craft, with the Quilters' Guild holding meetings and exhibitions.

119. *Square of* lacis *(darned net, or* filet brodé*):* The Pelican in her Piety. *The design is darned on to hand-knotted net. Taken from a sixteenth-century chart. Worked by Agnes M. Johnston, a student of Mrs Simpson ('Carita'), 1930.*

New materials suggested new techniques, or the new use of an old technique. Several Scottish linen firms, notably Donald Brothers of Dundee or N. Lockhart of Kirkcaldy, made an evenweave linen that was exported to Scandinavia for drawn fabric embroidery. It became available in Scotland, and using the same stitches employed on the fine muslin of Dresden work, this type of embroidery became immensely popular after the 1940s, to make tablemats, cloths, tea-cosies and lampshades. It was an ideal medium for the amateur, since the designs were geometrical and could be counted, while still demanding a wide repertoire of stitches and meticulous technique.

120. Tea-cosy. Cream watered silk with ribbon work roses and border; French knots and surface stitches in coloured silks. 1933. (Mrs M. Cross)

The linen also made a good foundation for blackwork.

Perhaps the most engaging and lively, and certainly one of the largest pieces made by an amateur this century, is the long panel designed and worked by Norah, Lady Ramsay Fairfax-Lucy, who died in 1980. A keen follower of the Jedforest Hunt, she made the hanging, which is roughly three feet deep and about twenty-five feet long, to hang around Jedburgh Town Hall on the occasion of the annual Hunt Ball. Worked on crash in surface and darning stitches, it shows the Hunt in full cry, against the background of the Border countryside. Every rider, and, it is said, every hound, is a portrait, with the figures of the embroideress and her sister complete with terrier, on foot beside their Landrover. Completed in 1960, the hanging is greatly treasured, and graced the

121. OPPOSITE Detail of a long hanging, showing members of the Jedforest Hunt. This large hanging, about twenty-five feet long, was designed and worked by Norah, Lady Ramsay Fairfax-Lucy, to hang around the Jedburgh Town Hall during the annual Hunt Ball. 1960. (The Master and members of the Jedforest Hunt)

122. Another detail of the hanging, showing the embroideress and her sister with terrier and Landrover. All the figures on the hanging are portraits. Surfaces stitches and darning on crash.

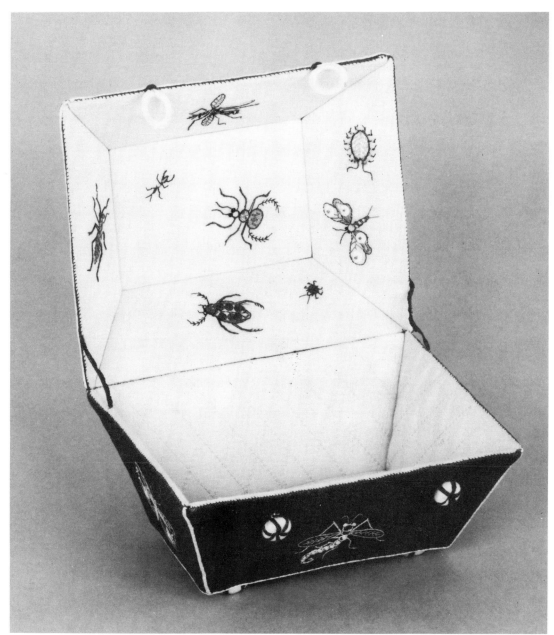

123. *OPPOSITE Panel:* Chimneys. *A study of chimneys and chimney pots by Margery Hyde, who died in 1979. Drawn fabric and blackwork stitches on Lockhart linen. 1970. 45 × 35 cm/17½ × 13½ in.* (The Trustees of the Royal Museum of Scotland)

124. *Embroidered box:* Pandora's Box, *designed and made by Anna Younger. The insects are all taken from a Ministry of Agriculture leaflet. Anna Younger is noted for her imaginative embroidered boxes and toys.* (The Trustees of the Royal Museum of Scotland)

hall on the occasion of the Centenary dinner of the Hunt in 1984. (Figs. 121 and 122.)

The amateur needlewoman in Scotland need no longer feel isolated, as her forbears did. Materials are available by post from specialist shops and exhibitions abound. She can attend classes to attain proficiency in design and technique up to the requirements of the City and Guilds of London examining body. In the country, the Scottish Women's Rural Institutes hold lively demonstrations and exhibit the best of members' work. The Royal Highland Show annually invites entries to its large handicraft exhibit, to be judged for excellence. The Embroiderers' Guild has some fifteen branches in Scotland, and includes among its members many talented amateurs as well as some of the most distinguished professional embroiderers working in Scotland today.

References
1. See p. 71.
2. Balcarres, Fife, where Henrietta Cumming had taught her charges how to draw embroidery designs.
3. Lord Falkland's pillow cover is now in the Victoria & Albert Museum, T.81–1924.
4. Shown in the exhibition *Needlework from Scottish Country Houses*, 1966, cat. no. 82.
5. Now in the collection of the Glasgow School of Art. I am indebted to Ailsa Tanner and Anne Paterson Wallace for information about Maggie Hamilton.
6. 'Carita', *Lacis (Filet brodé)*, Sampson Low, Marston & Co., London, 1909.

CHAPTER TWELVE

The New Professionals

Glasgow School of Art must justly be given the credit for the new approach to embroidery, not only in teaching methods, but especially in giving the subject its rightful place in the art and design course. Edinburgh Art College, the descendant of the Trustees' Academy, followed in 1914 with the appointment of Louisa M. Chart (1880–1963) as Teacher of Embroidery. Born at Hampton Court, where her father, a surveyor, was Master of Works, she had a strong sense of history. She trained at the Royal School of Needlework, and was one of the small group who founded the Embroiderers' Guild in 1906. She was an inspiring teacher with a rich sense of colour, and brought to Scotland not only the professional methods used at the Royal School, but a passionate interest in stitchery. Miss Chart insisted on her students exploring the infinite possibilities of stitches from the past and from other countries, contrasting their effect in tone, texture and thread.

As well as teaching, she undertook many commissions, maintaining a studio at her home in George Square. (Fig. 125.) She embroidered the Speaker's Faldstool in the House of Commons, undertook much heraldic work, especially banners, and supervised the tapestries and embroideries at Holyrood for many years. She completed a settee cover and covers for six chairs at the palace, adapting for the latter the cornucopia design of those worked by Jane Drummond, Duchess of Atholl, at Blair Castle. (See fig. 48.) She restored the three panels from Oxburgh Hall bought for Holyrood in 1961. One of these, the *Catte*, bears the cipher of Mary, Queen of Scots.[1] Her most memorable panel is the large *Edinburgh*

hanging (fig. 126) designed by her nephew, John R. Chart. It is a bird's-eye view of many of the city's landmarks, with affectionate portraits of some of its historic characters, worked in an astonishing variety of stitches on canvas.

Louisa Chart's influence spread far beyond Edinburgh. One of her first students, Dorothy Angus (1890–1979), after teaching for four years at the Carnegie Craft School at Dunfermline, was appointed to the staff of Gray's School of Art, Aberdeen. At Aberdeen, Dorothy Angus passed on the passion for stitchery she had imbibed from Miss Chart, coupled with a strong sense of design, and went on to inspire her own students to 'create a fusion between drawing, fabric and stitchery . . . a sense of vitality and line were the qualities she sought in her students' work'.[2]

Her energies were directed into her teaching. She remained at Gray's School of Art for thirty-five years. Unlike Louisa Chart, she undertook few large commissions, though Kathleen Whyte remembers an heraldic bedspread undertaken for Lord Glentanar, using cloth of gold and other rich fabrics. Her panels, *Fiery Furnace*, and even more, *War Impressions*, completed on the eve of the 1939 war, are apocalyptic in imagination with strongly controlled drawing. Dorothy Angus's most rewarding student was certainly Kathleen Whyte, whose dynamic teaching and achievements at Glasgow gave her immense pride.

An early assistant of Dorothy Angus was Isabel M. ('Belle') Barnet (1895–1983), who in 1922 became teacher of embroidery at the Dundee College of Art, now Duncan of Jordanstone College of Art. Her gentle style was a complete

125. *Louisa M. Chart in her private studio, George Square, Edinburgh, with work in progress, 1938. Foreground: a pipe banner worked to the order of HRH the Princess Royal. Nearby, the drawing of arms being worked for Lord Lovat on the occasion of his marriage. On the large frame three assistants work on the Edinburgh panel (fig. 126). Miss Chart stands by the coloured sketch; the full cartoon is in the background. (Mrs Katherine Chart)*

contrast to the trenchant humour of Dorothy Angus, and belied the strength of persuasion that could elicit the best out of the most unpromising student material. Like Dorothy Angus, she belonged to the exclusive Modern Embroidery Society that flourished from 1921 till 1939. Members of the Society showed panels in the large exhibition of modern and historical embroidery organized by

126. *Canvas work panel:* The Royal Burgh of Edinburgh, *designed by John R. Chart and worked by Louisa and Kate Chart and assistants, in a variety of canvas work stitches. The colouring is mostly blues and greens to suggest the city's misty atmosphere. 1938. 193 × 122 cm/76 × 48 in. (Mrs Katherine Chart)*

the Scottish Women's Rural Institutes in Edinburgh in 1934 at the Royal Scottish Academy.[3]

That same year, the Needlework Development Scheme, financed anonymously, was set up to encourage embroidery in Scotland and to raise the standard of design. Since the art colleges were regarded as the spearhead of this aim, the organisation of the Scheme was entrusted to the four art colleges in Aberdeen, Dundee, Edinburgh and Glasgow. A collection of some nine hundred foreign and British embroideries was formed, and both Dorothy Angus and Louisa Chart, as well as Agnes McCredie in Glasgow, took part in finding items for the collection, especially the work of foreign contemporaries. At first restricted to the art and domestic science colleges in Scotland, the Scheme was extended, after 1944, to make it available to schools and Women's Institutes throughout Britain. Until 1961, when it closed, the Needlework Development Scheme, under its successive organizers, Kay Kohler, Ulla Kockum, Dorothy Allsop and Iris Hills, produced attractive leaflets, slides and portfolios, in order to improve the standard of design.[4]

Meanwhile, the distinction between amateur and professional has continued. Although Mrs

127. *The Cardross Panels, designed and worked by Hannah Frew Paterson for Cardross Church of Scotland. The centre panel embodies a plain wooden cross on a hill, around which mankind gathers. Below are medallions symbolizing the cell, the foetus and the babe. Left is the landscape beyond Cardross, with bands of plant life below. Right is the Clyde estuary, with mineral strata. Each panel measures 202 × 112.5 cm/79½ × 44 in.* (Cardross Church)

Newbery opened her classes to any woman interested in serious embroidery, and Ann Macbeth, to the end of her life, preached that anyone could make her own design from simple leaf shapes or other units, both of them, like William Morris, were always willing to draw out designs for others to work. On the other hand, full-time students of the art colleges, selected for their talent in draughtmanship and trained as artists, have rightly regarded embroidery as a medium, like glass, stone or metal, in which to express their artistic imagination. The distinction between amateur and professional has been emphasized since the art colleges were accepted by the Council for National Academic Awards to prepare their students to honours standard (BA) and all four Scottish colleges came into line with the rest of Britain.

However, Colleges of Further Education, such

174

as Cardonald College, Glasgow and Telford College, Edinburgh are now able to offer part-time courses in embroidery to mature students without qualifications leading to the examinations of the City and Guilds of London Institute.[5]

The professional embroiderers of today, those students who graduate from an art college with a degree, are scarcely able to support themselves by embroidery alone, which is more time-consuming than painting, as well as perhaps less regarded. Most of them have to work in other fields, such as designing, or, if they have the vocation, teaching. This gives some opportunity to develop their own work for exhibition and to undertake commis-

128. Detail of the right-hand panel. Fossils and minerals. Layers of appliqué, gold and embroidery on a firm cotton foundation. An actual piece of fossilized wood is incorporated. (Hannah Frew Paterson)

sions. Hannah Frew Paterson, for instance, is a part-time lecturer at the Glasgow School of Art. She was a student of Kathleen Whyte from 1963 to 1967 and won the Newbery medal in 1967. In 1981 she was commissioned to make an embroidered panel for Cardross Church of Scotland, in memory of Lorna Hendry.

The panel developed into a triptych, that domi-

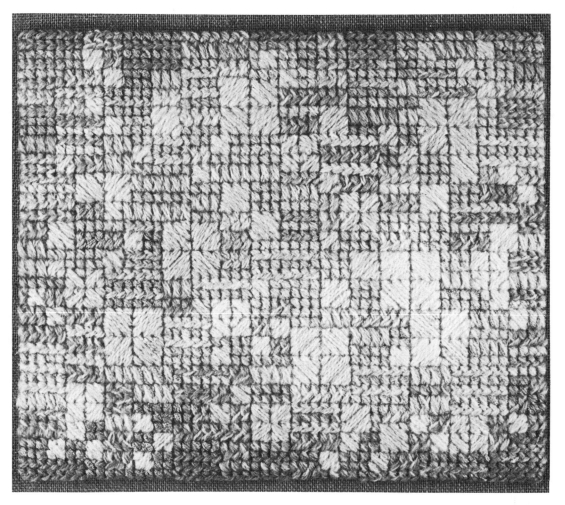

129. *Panel:* Field II, *designed and worked by Veronica Togneri, 1978. Textured canvas work; cross stitches and satin stitch in silks and wools of greens, orange and yellows. Inspired by a visit to Hardwick Hall.* 12×14 *cm*/$4\frac{3}{4} \times 5\frac{1}{2}$ *in. (Veronica Togneri)*

nates the east end of the church, and took over three years to complete. It is deeply symbolic, with a plain wooden cross, that has been in the church for many years, at the apex of a hill, with mankind gathered beneath. Below are three medallions representing human life itself in the cell, the foetus, and the babe. On one side, beneath the hilly local landscape, lie bands of plant life; on the other is

depicted the view across the Clyde, with strata of minerals below. (Figs. 127 and 128.) From the entrance to the church, the panels appear as an arrestingly simple, glowing hill shape surmounted by a cross. As one draws nearer, the rich textural details of appliqué and stitchery are revealed.[6]

Veronica Togneri is a distinguished freelance, who, like Hannah Frew Paterson, belongs to the Glasgow School of Art Embroidery and Tapestry Society, and exhibits regularly. She has had her own weaving workshop on the island of Colonsay since 1962. In 1983 she moved to Tomintoul, Banffshire. Although primarily interested in embroidery she supports herself by weaving, of a high

130. Panel: Night Sky, *designed and worked by Jennifer Hex, 1983. Darning technique using silk threads on linen in shades of black, white and greys. 45 × 36 cm/17¾ × 14 in. (Jennifer Hex)*

standard and immaculate technique. She was Artist in Residence at the University of Sussex in 1978. In 1983 she was awarded a Scottish Development Craft Fellowship, which gave her the freedom to spend a year developing a personal and opulent form of patchwork: small squares of silk in a subtle range of colour, sometimes combined with lettering. Her embroidery is strongly disciplined, and she explores traditional techniques, such as canvas work, imbued with rich colour. (Fig. 129.)

Jennifer Hex was also a graduate of the Glasgow School of Art, specializing in printmaking. She trained as a teacher and taught in schools in Ayrshire and Argyll. It was only in 1970 that she began to take a serious interest in embroidery. In 1980 she decided to leave teaching and become a freelance embroiderer and part-time weaver. Her panels show rigorous draughtsmanship, but are imbued with a lyrical approach to colour and texture that can be achieved only in embroidery. (Fig. 130.)

Another artist who was drawn to embroidery by its texture, unobtainable in painting, is Alison King. She graduated MA (Hons) in Fine Art at Edinburgh University in 1969, in a course run in

131. Highland Triptych (Torridon), *designed and worked by Alison King, 1984. A romantic landscape in appliqué of sheer materials and velvets, some padded, with hand and machine embroidery. 130 × 72 cm/51 × 28 in. (Alison King)*

conjunction with the College of Art. She belongs to the '62 Group of the Embroiderers' Guild, and is the founder-chairman of the New Scottish Embroidery Group. She teaches part-time and undertakes many private commissions. Much of her embroidery is three-dimensional ('soft sculpture') and often light-hearted, as she feels that embroidery can often be taken too seriously. Her panels show a painterly approach, with a widening awareness of the infinite possibilities of working with textiles. One work, a triptych, was done for her family. (Fig. 131.) Labelled *Torridon*, a remote part of Ross and Cromarty in the north-west of Scotland, it shows a tawny landscape under a stormy sky, apparently empty, until one sees the tiny figures of cyclists battling against the wind.

A large textile hanging was commissioned by the architect Norman Hunter, for the new building of the Poultry Research Centre of the University of Edinburgh. One of the conditions laid down was that all the poultry depicted should be recognizable breeds. A striking collage was designed and worked by Inga Blair, trained in Sweden, who obtained the City and Guilds certificate and is married to a Scottish architect. The panel (fig. 132) shows a glimpse of the building, with test tubes,

132. *Collage:* The World of Poultry, *1981, designed and worked by Inga Blair for the Poultry Research Centre, Roslin, Midlothian. All the poultry are recognizable breeds. Appliqué, quilting, soft sculpture and canvas work on a background of cotton/linen twill. 300 × 250 cm/78 × 98¼ in. (*The Poultry Research Centre/Inga Blair*)

yolks and chromosomes, as well as recognizable decorative breeds. This won the 'Art in Architecture' award in 1981, given every three years by the Saltire Society.

Mary Johnstone is an artist who specializes in gold work. She trained at the Royal School of

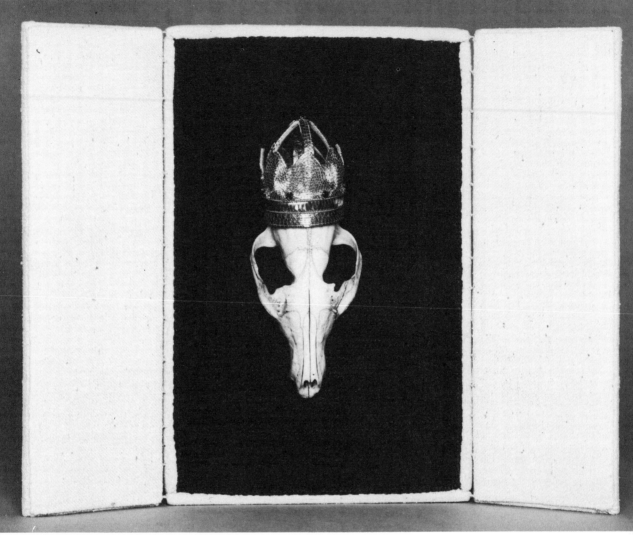

133. Panel in a fabric-lined box: King Tod, *designed and worked by Mary Johnstone. Bleached fox's skull surmounted by a stiffened gold crown in Japanese and plate gold. The box measures 33 × 23 × 10 cm/13 × 9 × 3¾ in.* (Mary Johnstone)

Needlework, London, and the Camberwell School of Arts and Crafts. She became technical editor of *The Needlewoman* before it ceased publication in 1939, and married William Johnstone, the distinguished painter who was Principal of the Central School of Arts and Crafts. They retired to a farm in his native Borders of Scotland, and it was there that she decided to work with gold again, a technique 'as far removed from hay and turnips and feeding cattle as possible'. She designs jewellery such as torques and earrings, chessmen and panels. Because she works only with precious materials, the panels tend to be small cabinet pieces. Some, incorporating the bleached skulls of small animals dug up on their farm, have an occult air of mystery. (Fig. 133.)

Finally, the wheel has come full circle, and there are again male embroiderers, as there were in the past in Scotland. Malcolm M. Lochhead, trained at the Glasgow School of Art (1966–70) and now lecturer in Design at Queen's College, Glasgow, was commissioned in 1972 to design a cover and kneelers for the shrine of St Mungo in Glasgow's medieval cathedral. The cover, in richly shimmering patchwork, is of Laudian shape, transforming the tomb into an altar. It is punctuated by six square kneelers, set like jewels around the tomb, worked on canvas in dark wools and lurex yarn. The cover and kneelers were worked by thirty-four members of the Embroiderers' Guild under his direction.[7]

This wholly personal selection gives some idea of the range of work undertaken on commission today. Indeed, the numbers of trained embroiderers now working in Scotland must be greater than at any time during the centuries covered by this book. They are the new professionals, skilled draughtsmen, graduates of the Scottish art colleges and other establishments in Britain. They are textile artists, continually experimenting with techniques and pushing back the boundaries of what was hitherto considered as needlework, incorporating in addition weaving, knitting, lace, paper and metal. They are the innovators, displaying their work in exhibitions, ready to be considered for commissions by architects and others, as well as offering inspiration to the talented amateur. Many of them, even more generous with their talents, teach in schools or in evening classes, or to the Embroiderers' Guild, thus ensuring that embroidery in Scotland flourishes as never before.

References
1. L.M. Chart, 'Mary Queen of Scots Panels', *Embroidery* Vol XII, no.2, Summer 1961, p. 50. Miss Chart retired from the Edinburgh College of Art in 1947 and was succeeded by Agnes M. Kindberg, who added Dress Design to the curriculum.
2. K. Whyte, 'Dorothy Angus in Aberdeen', *Embroidery* Vol. XXIV, no.3, Autumn 1973, p. 73.
3. SWRI, National Exhibition of Needlework in the Royal Scottish Academy Galleries, Edinburgh, 16 Oct. to 3 Nov. 1934. Other members of the Modern Embroidery Society who exhibited were Mabel Dawson RSW and Penelope Beaton.
4. R. Oddy, *Embroideries from the Needlework Development Scheme*, Royal Scottish Museum, 1965.
5. I am indebted to Mr Angus R. Gallon HMI for this information.
6. H. Frew, *Three Dimensional Embroidery*, Van Nostrand Reinhold, 1975. 'Methods for designing Laid Work', *Embroidery* Vol. XXVII, no. 4, Winter 1976, p. 110.
7. M.M. Lochhead, 'Religious Symbolism' *Embroidery* Vol. XXIII, no. 4, Winter 1972, p. 110. 'Symbols of Christ', *Embroidery* Vol. XXIV, no.1, Spring 1973, p. 23. A.R. Kennedy, 'A gift of Embroidery', *Embroidery* Vol. XXIV, no.3, Autumn 1973, p. 80.
   See also: C. Howard, *Twentieth Century Embroidery in Britain* 1964–77, Batsford, 1984. D. Springall, *Twelve British Embroiderers*, Gakken Press, 1984. (Obtainable only from the Embroiderers' Guild.)

Appendix I

*Embroideries for the Church of Scotland designed
and worked by staff and students of the Glasgow
School of Art*

Kathleen Whyte

1950	Queen's Park Church, Glasgow	Pulpit fall: *Lamb of God*
1950	St Martin's Church, Port Glasgow	Pulpit fall: long red silk
1950	Fernhill and Cathkin Church, Glasgow	Pulpit fall: white and silver
1950	Bardainney Church, Hamilton	Pulpit fall: green *Dove*
1952	Shawlands Old Parish Church, Glasgow	White linen Communion cloth
1960	(Private)	White pulpit fall: *Live Coal*
1960	St Brendan's Church, Bute	Pulpit fall: *Targe*
1960	Glasgow	Pulpit fall and markers: *Chi Rho*
1964	Allan Park Church, Stirling	Pulpit fall: *Burning Bush*
1972	Mayfield Church, Edinburgh	Cloth: *Converging on the Hand of God*
1973	Gourock Old Parish Church	Pulpit fall: *Holy Spirit*
1973	London	White and silver hanging
1973	Cathcart Church, Glasgow	Pulpit fall: red *Trinity*
1976	Gourock Old Parish Church	*Arms of Gourock*
1978	Netherlee Church, Glasgow	Figure for vestibule: 5½ feet
1979	Cathcart South Church, Glasgow	Lectern fall: *Palm Sunday*
1980	Stenton Church, Midlothian	Memorial fall for Dorothy and Mabs Angus
1982	Westerton Church, Glasgow	Pulpit fall: *Rainbow and Dove*
1984	Prestonkirk, East Lothian	Pulpit fall: *City set on a Hill*

Ann Hunter

1960	St Giles Cathedral, Edinburgh	Pulpit fall: white

Groups of students from Glasgow School of Art

1963	Glasgow University Chapel	Four pulpit falls
1965	West Church of St Nicholas, Aberdeen	Three pulpit falls
1965	St Columba's Church, Glasgow	Pulpit fall
1965	Scotstoun West Parish Church Glasgow	Pulpit fall
1973	Sherbrook St Gilbert's Church Glasgow	Panel for Communion table and scarf
1974	Kintore Parish Church, Aberdeenshire	Four pulpit falls
1979	Renfield St Stephen's Church Glasgow	Pulpit fall: *Tree of Life*
1980	Mid Kirk of Greenock	Pulpit fall

Hannah Frew Paterson

1963	Chapelton Parish Church	Two pulpit falls
1964	Allan Park Church, Stirling	Scarf for Communion table
1968	Kirkton Parish Church, Carluke	Pulpit fall
1972	Colmonell Church	Pulpit fall and markers
1975	Mansefield Church, Kilwinning	Pulpit fall, pulpit back panel
		Three sets of Bible markers
1977	Gorbals Parish Church, Glasgow	Pulpit fall
1981	Cardross Parish Church, Dunbartonshire	Triple panel behind the Communion table, total size 12 ft x 7 ft
		Pulpit fall and markers
1984	Wellington Church, Glasgow	Pulpit fall: *The Cup* – to celebrate church's centenary
1984	Old Parish Church of Hamilton	Pulpit fall to celebrate 250th anniversary
		Bible markers
		Communion table scarf
		Kneelers
		Minister's stole

Malcolm Lochhead and members of the Embroiderers' Guild (Glasgow)

| 1972 | Glasgow Cathedral | Cover for St Mungo's tomb, kneelers |

Malcolm Lochhead

1970	Glasgow Cathedral	Pulpit fall
1972	St Pauls' Church, Johnstone	Pulpit fall
1974	Kilbirnie Church, Ayrshire	Communion table scarf
1974	Edinburgh University	Minister's stole
1977	Port Glasgow	Pulpit fall
1979	Nurses' Chapel, Glasgow Cathedral	Eight chair seats
1982	St John's Church, Paisley	Pulpit fall: *Eagle*

Marilyn McGregor

1967	Sherbrook St Gilbert's Church, Glasgow	Pulpit fall
1968	Lorne Street Church, Campbeltown	Pulpit back cloth: three panels, total size 10 ft x 7 ft
		Pulpit fall and markers: *Burning Bush*
1968	Barlanark Church, Glasgow	Communion table cloth
1979	St Margaret's Church, Greenock	Pulpit fall
1982	Killearn Church	Pulpit fall
1984	Kilbarchan East Church	Pulpit fall
1985	Methodist Hall, Paisley	Pulpit fall
		Lectern fall

Crissie White

| 1980 | New Kilpatrick Parish Church, Bearsden | Pulpit fall: *Crown of Thorns* (Lenten) – on view six weeks before Easter |

| 1982 | Renfield St Stephen's Church, Glasgow | Trinity pulpit fall – green – *Father, Son and Holy Spirit* |
| 1984 | Moderator of General Assembly Revd John Paterson, St Paul's Church, Milngavie | Stole, commissioned by Presbytery of Dumbarton |

Joan Milroy

1978	Dunkeld Fellowship	Stole
1980	St Mary's Church, Haddington	Stole
1981	St Andrew's Church, Blantyre	Pulpit fall
1982	Dundee Parish Church	Stole
1982	St Blane's Church, Dunblane	Pulpit fall
1982	St Leonard's Church, Ayr	Pulpit fall
1983	St Andrew's Church, Ayr (Boys' Brigade)	Pulpit fall

Appendix II

Places to see Scottish embroidery mentioned in this book

The Palace of Holyroodhouse, Edinburgh
Blair Castle, Blair Atholl, Perthshire
Drum Castle, Aberdeenshire (NTS)
Castle Fraser, Inverurie, Aberdeenshire (NTS)
Drumlanrig, Dumfriesshire
The Georgian House, Edinburgh (NTS)
Glamis Castle, Angus

Haddo House, Aberdeenshire (NTS)
Hopetoun House, West Lothian
Hardwick Hall, Derbyshire (NT)
Lennoxlove, East Lothian
Mellerstain, Berwickshire
Oxburgh Hall, Norfolk (NT)
Traquair, Innerleithen, Peeblesshire

(NTS: National Trust for Scotland. NT: National Trust for England and Wales)
Times of opening should always be checked before visiting.

Museums

Edinburgh: The Royal Museum of Scotland
Glasgow:　 The Burrell Collection
　　　　　　Kelvingrove Museum

Most of the Scottish museums have collections of embroidery, especially Ayrshire work, but not always on display.

Churches

Aberdeen, St Nicholas Kirk
Glasgow, St Mungo's Cathedral

Churches belonging to the Church of Scotland are closed except for services.

Index

Aberdeen
    Cathedral 12
    Gray's School of Art 147, 171
    St Nicholas Kirk 64–7
Aberdeen, Countess of 82
Adam, Robert 80
Allan, David 80, 96
Allsop, Dorothy 173
Angus, Dorothy 147, 171
Anne, Queen 45
Arbroath 147
Archdeacon, Miss 126
Archers, Company of 48
Argyll, Duchess of 57
Argyll, Duke of 162
Arniston, Midlothian 24, 80
Arthur, Anne Knox 144
Artois, Comte d' (Charles X of France) 73
Ashburnham House, Sussex 55
Atholl, Charlotte, Duchess of 71
Atholl, Jane Drummond, Duchess of 71, 171
Ayr 98

Baillie, Lady Grisell 47, 107, 109–13, 156
Balcarres, Fife 89
Balhousie Castle, Perth 24
Balloch (Taymouth Castle) 24, 107
Belfast, Ulster Museum 113
Belon, Pierre 40
Biggar 130
Blair, Inga 178
Blair Castle 55, 107, 165
Bowie, Mrs and Miss 127
Bothwell, Earl of 13, 32
British Association for the Advancement of Science 104
Brown, Alexander 101
Brown, Sharp & Co. 103

Bruce, Sir George 54
Bruges 15, 54
Brussels 156
Buccleuch, Duchess of 126
Buccleuch, Duke of 29
Buckingham Palace 73

Camberwell, School of Arts and Crafts 170
Campbell of Glenorchy, Sir Colin 24
Campbell of Glenorchy, Dame Julian 25
Carmichael, Isabella 127
Charles I 44
Charles Edward Stuart, Prince 75, 87
Chart, John R. 171
Chart, Louisa M. 147, 171
Chatsworth 75
Chipchase & Lambert 71
Clark, Edith 164
Cochrane & Brown 103
Cock, H. 30
Cockburn, Mrs 89
Collie, John 75
Colquhoun, Adam 13
Condé, Servais de 12, 19, 34
Crawford, Constance, Countess of 155
Crawford, Mary, Countess of 155
Cullen House, Banffshire 54
Cumming, Henrietta 89, 93
Cumming, James 89

Dalhousie, Marchioness of 123
Dalhousie, Mary, Countess of 155
Dalkeith 98
Dallas, Helen 55, 89
Dalzell, Mrs (Jamieson) 101
Darnley, Henry, Lord 32
Dauphin, *see* Francis II
Delany, Mrs 84

Donald Bros 44, 165
Douglas, Gavin, Bishop 15
Drum Castle 71
Drummond of Comrie 14
Drummond, William of Hawthornden 41
Dundee, Duncan of Jordanstone College of Art 149, 171
Dunfermline, Carnegie Craft School 171

Edinburgh
   Art College 147, 171
   Caroline Park 57
   Castle 13
   Georgian House 80
   Guild of Hammermen 13, 117
   Guild of Tailors 41
   Telford College 175
   University, Poultry Research Centre 178
Eglinton, Earl of 98
Elesmere, Nicolas 41
Elizabeth, Queen of England 32, 39, 41
Elizabeth, HM the Queen Mother 74, 149, 153
Elphinstone, Lady 155
Embroiderers' Guild 170, 171, 181
Embroiderers, male
   Beaton [Betoun], William 21, 42
   Cuming, James 48
   Forrester, Thomas 44
   Gordon, Adam 44
   Haddington, Earl of 156
   Lochhead, Malcolm M. 181
   Miller, Ninian 19, 21
   Moffat, Menzies 130
   Monro, John 133
   Oudry, Pierre 32, 38, 60, 171
   Plouvart, Charles 38
   Porteus, Robert 44
   Robertson, David 133
   Ruffini, Luigi 93–8
   Scott, W. Schomberg 162
   Tod, Hew 44
   White (Quhyte) family 42, 44
   Young, John 13

Falkland palace 32, 162
Fetternear, Aberdeenshire 15
Finlay, Kirkman 98
Forbes, Lord 29
Fordyce, Sir Alexander 90
Francis II, of France 12, 19

Fraser, Castle 80
Fraser, Miss Elyza 80

Gardner, Elizabeth 113–14
Gauguin, Jane 126
Glasgow 98, 102, 105, 113
   Cardonald College 175
   Kelvingrove Museum 133
   Lady Artists' Club 162
   Queen's College 181
   St Mungo's Cathedral 13, 181
   School of Art 138–50, 171, 175
Glamis Castle 60, 63
Glentanar, Lord 171
Graham, Alexander 15
Grant, Anne 75
Gordon Castle 119
Gordon, Lord Adam 75, 153
Gordon, Henrietta, Duchess of 75
Gordon, William, cabinetmaker 71
Gosford House 75
Guthrie, Sir James 161

Haddo House 63, 80
Hamilton, Anne, Duchess of 53
Hamilton, Maggie (Mrs A.N.Paterson) 158–9
Hamilton Palace 60, 87
Hardwick Hall 32
Haustan, Gerard de, wife of 13
Heemskerke, M. 67
Helensburgh 161
Henry II of France 32
Henry VIII of England 32
Hex, Jennifer 177
Hill, Thos, haberdasher 87
Hills, Iris 173
Hog, Lady Mary 80
Holyroodhouse, palace of 12, 32, 41
   furnishings 71, 75, 153, 171
Hopetoun, Countesses of 87
Houston and Killallan parish 97
Hume, Katherine 53
Huntly, Earl of 12, 19

Inverary Castle 119
Inverkeithing, Fife 107
Iona 162
Ireland 103

James V of Scotland 32

James VI of Scotland (James I of Great Britain) 21, 28, 32, 41, 42
James VII of Scotland (James II of Great Britain) 44
Jamesone, Mary 64
Jamieson, Mrs 98
Jedforest Hunt 167
Johnstone, Mary 179
Jonson, Ben 41

Kellie Castle, Fife 158
Kilbryde Castle, Perthshire 28
King, Alison 177
Kingsdale, Fife 119
Kirkintilloch 96
Kirkwall, Orkney 53
Knox, John 12
Kockum, Ulla 173
Kohler, Kay 173

Lancashire 105
Lauderdale, Duke of 80
Lennoxlove 63
Leveson-Gower, Lady Rose 73
Liberty & Co. 144
Lindsay, Lady Anne and Lady Margaret 89
Linlithgow, palace of 21, 28, 32
Lochhead, Malcolm M. 181
Lochleven 21, 29, 32, 34, 87
Lockhart, Mrs James 87
Lockhart, N., of Kirkcaldy 165
Logan, Katherine 111
London 44
    Broderers' Company 41, 42, 50
Lorimer, Louise 158
Lorimer, Sir Robert 158
Lotherton Hall, Yorkshire 68

Macbeth, Ann 142–4
McCredie, Agnes 145
McConnell, E. & C. 127
Macdonald, Frances 138, 144
Macdonald, Margaret 138, 158
Mackay, Ian Aberach 15
Mayfield Church, Edinburgh 149
Mair, John & Co. 130
Mann, Kathleen 145
Marchmont, Earl of 45
Mar, Countess of 80
Mary, HM Queen 73, 153
Mary de Guise 32

Mary, Queen of Scots 12, 19, 32–40, 60, 87, 123, 133, 164, 171
Maxwell-Stuart, Flora 155
Melfort, Earl of 45
Mellerstain 47, 71, 80, 133
Menteith, Earl of 28
Menzies, May 109
Metropolitan Museum, New York 24, 27
Modern Embroidery Society 172
Montgomerie, Lady Mary 98
Montrose, lace school 87
Monymusk, Aberdeenshire 55, 75
Morris, J.A. 104
Morton, Countess of 53
Morton, Earls of 29
Müller, A. 126
Murray, Lady Evelyn Stuart 156
Musselburgh 98

Nairne, Lady 10
National Library of Scotland 84
Naughton 55
Needlework Development Scheme 173
Newbery, Mrs 138–42, 174
Newliston 80
Norfolk, Duke of 39

Ogilvie, Lady 21
Old Cumnock 108
Oliphant, Jane, Countess of Hopetoun 164
Oliphant, Janet, of Gask 84
Oliphant, Katherine (Dundas) 24
Oxburgh Hall, Norfolk 32, 38, 60, 171

Paisley 95, 96
Pascall, Elizabeth Coates 71
Paterson, Hannah Frew 176
Patterdale, Cumbria 144
Perth, Duke of 45
Perthshire 21, 47
Philadelphia 71
Picardy 95
Prestonhall, Midlothian 75

Quilters' Guild 164

Ramsey Fairfax-Lucy, Nora 167
Renfrew 95, 96
Robson, Adam 163
Rollo, Lord 47

Royal Highland Show 170
Royal Museum of Scotland 25, 28, 46, 55, 80, 87,
    107, 113, 161
Royal Repository for the Work of Indigent
    Gentlewomen 164
Royal School of Needlework, London 133, 171,
    180
Ruthven family 24

St Esprit, Order of 45
Salomon, Bernard 24
Saltire Society 179
Saxony 126
Schaw, John 89
Scottish Handcraft Circle 164
Scottish Womens' Rural Institutes 170, 173
Scone Palace 30, 60
Sewell, Samuel 54
Sheffield 34
Shrewsbury, Countess of (Bess of Hardwick) 40
Shrewsbury, Earl of 34
Simpson, Mrs ('Carita') 164
Sissinghurst 130
Skinner, Mrs Jeannie 158
Soane, Sir John's Museum 80
Spalding of Ashintully 48
Standish, Lora 119
Steel, Mary 98
Stirling 32
Strang, J. 104
Strathmore, Cecilia, Countess of 153
Strathmore, Patrick, Earl of 62
Stuart, Lady Lucy and Lady Anne 82
Sussex, University of 177

Swanson, Margaret 144
Switzerland 105

Thistle, Order of 45
Togneri, Veronica, 176
Tomintoul, Banffshire 176
Tongue, Sutherland 15
Traquair, Earl of 82
Traquair House 55, 62, 155
Traquair, Phoebe 136
Trustees Academy, Edinburgh 93, 133, 171
Tweeddale, Marchioness, 123
Tyninghame, East Lothian 60, 156

Vaughan, Edward 75
Victoria, HM Queen 102, 123, 130
Victoria and Albert Museum 114, 133

Webster, Mrs 133
Wemyss Castle, Fife 55, 68, 80
Wemyss, James, Earl of 48, 68
Wemyss, Janet, Countess of 68
Wemyss, Miss (Lady Henry Grosvenor) 133–4
Wemyss School of Needlework 133, 136
Wemyss, Lady Victoria 136, 156
West Monkland 97
White, Crissie 149
Whyte, Kathleen 145–9, 171, 175
Wierix, Jean 31
William III and Mary 45
Wylie, Alexander 103

Yorke, James Whiting 80
Younger, Rachel, Lady 163